UNDERSTANDING STOCKS

Michael Sincere

McGraw·Hill

New York   Chicago   San Francisco   Lisbon   London   Madrid   Mexico City
Milan   New Delhi   San Juan   Seoul   Singapore   Sydney   Toronto

The *McGraw·Hill* Companies

*In memory of a wonderful and remarkable man,
my late father, Charles Sincere, Jr., who loved the Cubs,
stiff martinis, and hamburgers.*

Library of Congress Cataloging-in-Publication Data

Sincere, Michael.
    Understanding stocks/ by Michael Sincere.
        p. cm.
        ISBN 0-07-140913-0 (pbk. : alk. paper)
        1. Stocks. I. Title.
    HG4551.S564 2003
    332.63'22—dc21   2002155429

11 12 13 14 15   DOC/DOC   0 9 8

ISBN 0-07-140913-0

This publication is designed to provide accurate and authoritative information in regard to the subject matter covered. It is sold with the understanding that neither the author nor the publisher is engaged in rendering legal, accounting, or other professional service. If legal advice or other expert assistance is required, the services of a competent professional person should be sought.
    *—From a declaration of principles jointly adopted by a committee of the
American Bar Association and a committee of publishers.*

 This book is printed on recycled, acid-free paper containing a minimum of 50% recycled de-inked fiber.

McGraw-Hill books are available at special quantity discounts to use as premiums and sales promotions, or for use in corporate training programs. For more information, please write to the Director of Special Sales, Professional Publishing, McGraw-Hill, Two Penn Plaza, New York, NY 10121-2298. Or contact your local bookstore.

Contents

Acknowledgments   v

Introduction   vii

PART ONE

WHAT YOU NEED TO KNOW FIRST

1   Welcome to the Stock Market   3

2   Stocks: Not Your Only Investment   19

3   How to Classify Stocks   29

4   Fun Things You Can Do (with Stocks)   37

5   Understanding Stock Prices   49

6   Where to Buy Stocks   55

PART TWO

MONEY-MAKING STRATEGIES

7   Want to Make Money Slowly?
    Try These Investment Strategies   69

8   Want to Make Money Fast?
    Try These Trading Strategies   77

PART THREE

FINDING STOCKS TO BUY AND SELL

9   It's Really Fundamental:
     Introduction to Fundamental Analysis   89

10   Fundamental Analysis: Tools and Tactics   97

11   Let's Get Technical:
     Introduction to Technical Analysis   107

12   Technical Analysis: Tools and Tactics   131

13   The Psychology of Stocks:
     Introduction to Sentiment Analysis   141

PART FOUR

UNCOMMON ADVICE

14   What Makes Stocks Go Up or Down   149

15   Why Investors Lose Money   157

16   What I Really Think about the Stock Market   171

     Index   189

Acknowledgments

I'd like to give special thanks:

To Stephen Isaacs and Jeffrey Krames at McGraw-Hill for once again giving me the opportunity to do what I love most, and to Pattie Amoroso for helping me put the pieces together to produce a book.

To my researcher, Maria Schmidt, who found the answer to nearly everything I asked; Tine Claes, who never fails to find something that needs improvement; and Lois Sincere, who has truly mastered the idiosyncrasies of the English language.

To Tom Reid, an economic consultant, for helping to make the most complicated financial concepts seem easy; student Bailey Brooks for helping with editing; Dan Larkin, CEO and senior consultant for Larkin Industries, Inc., for his extremely insightful suggestions and comments; Mike Fredericks, Brad Northern, and Howard Kornstein for their thoughtful financial analysis and insights; Colleen McCluney for her encouragement and patience; and Oksana Smirnova for her inspiration and enthusiasm.

To the hardworking and friendly staff at Barnes & Noble bookstore and Starbucks in Boca Raton, Florida.

Finally, to my friends, family, and acquaintances:

Idil Baran, Krista Barth, Bruce Berger, Andrew Brownsword, Sylvia Coppersmith, Lourdes Fernandez-Vidal, Alice Fibigrova, Joe Harwood, Jackie Krasner, Johan Nilsson, Joanne Pessin, Hal Plotkin, Anna Ridolfo, Tim Schenden, Tina Siegismund, Luigi Silverstri, Alex Sincere, Debra Sincere, Miriam Sincere, Richard Sincere, Harvey

Small, Bob Spector, Lucie Stejskalova, Deron Wagner, and Kerstin Woldorf.

For additional reading, I recommend the following books (in any order):

A Beginner's Guide to Short-Term Trading by Toni Turner
Reminiscences of a Stock Operator by Edwin Lefevre
Understanding Options by Michael Sincere
Trading for a Living by Dr. Alexander Elder
Market Wizards by Jack D. Schwager
How To Make Money in Stocks by William J. O'Neil
The Intelligent Investor by Benjamin Graham
One Up on Wall Street by Peter Lynch
Stock Trader's Almanac by Jeffrey A. Hirsch
Technical Analysis of Stock Trends by D. Edwards
Technical Analysis of the Financial Markets by John J. Murphy
The Essays of Warren Buffett by Warren E. Buffett
When Genius Failed by Roger Lowenstein
Options as a Strategic Investment by Lawrence McMillan
Confessions of a Street Addict by James Cramer

Introduction

This book will be different.

Thousands of books have already been written about the stock market, many of them technical and tedious. Before I wrote this book, I was amazed that so many boring books had been written about such a fascinating subject. Just like you, I hate reading books that put me to sleep by the second chapter. That is why I was so determined to write an entertaining, easy-to-read, and educational book about the market.

I wanted to write a book that I can hand to you and say, "Read everything in this book if you want to learn quickly about stocks." You don't have to be a dummy, idiot, or fool to understand the market. You also don't have to be a genius. After you read this book, you will realize that understanding stocks is not that hard. (The hard part is making money, but we'll get to that later.)

I also don't think you should have to wade through 300 pages to learn about the market. Too many books on stocks are as thick as college textbooks and not nearly as exciting. Even though this book is short, it is packed with information about investing and trading. I did my best to make sure that you would have a short and easy read.

I wrote this book because I wanted you to know the truth.

As I was writing, a corporate crime wave was sweeping across America. Dozens of corporations were accused of cheating people out of millions of dollars. It upset me that so many investors have become victims of the stock market. It seems as if the name of the game is enticing individual investors into the market so that they can be duped out of all their money.

The insiders on Wall Street and in many corporations understand the rules and know how to use them to lure you into putting your money in the market. In this book, I promise to tell you the truth about how the markets operate. Without that knowledge, you hardly have a chance to win against the pros who do business on Wall Street. They go to work every day with one goal in mind: to take money away from you.

Because the stock market is a brutal game that is often rigged in favor of the house, you should be quite sure you know what you're up against before you invest your first dime. Unfortunately, you can't win unless you know how to play. One goal of this book is to educate you about how the markets operate so that you can decide for yourself whether you want to participate. By the end of the book, you'll know the players, the rules, and the vocabulary.

I don't want to scare you, just prepare you.

After my unsettling introduction, you may decide that you don't want to have anything to do with the stock market. In my opinion, that would be a mistake. First of all, understanding the market can help you make financial decisions. The stock market is the core of our financial system, and understanding how it works will guide you for the rest of your life. In addition, the market often acts as a crystal ball, showing where the economy is headed.

This book is also ideal for people who still aren't sure whether to participate in the market. By the last chapter, you should have a better idea as to whether investing directly in the stock market makes sense for you. Although I can't make any promises, it is also possible that understanding the market will help you build wealth. Perhaps you will put your money into the stock market, but I will give you other invest-ment ideas.

How to Read this Book

If you are a first-time investor (and even if you're not), I suggest you begin by reading the first, second, and fourth sections. This will give you an overview of the market (Parts One and Two), and ways to avoid losing money (Part Four). Because Part Three is the most challenging and technical, it should be saved for last. As a special bonus, at the end of the last chapter I reveal a trading strategy that has not lost money during the last eight calendar years. I think you'll be intrigued by this simple but effective strategy that contradicts the advice included in nearly every other investment book.

I wish you the best of luck. I sincerely hope you find that learning about stocks is an enlightening experience, one that you will always remember.

PART ONE

WHAT YOU NEED TO KNOW FIRST

1

Welcome to the Stock Market

You may be surprised, but the market is not as difficult to understand as you might think. By the time you finish reading this chapter, you should have enough knowledge of the market to allow you to sail through the rest of the book. The trick is to learn about the market in small steps, which is exactly how I present the information to you.

The Stock Market: The Biggest Auction in the World

Think of the stock market as a huge auction or swap meet (some might call it a flea market) where people buy and sell pieces of paper called stock. On one side, you have the owners of corporations who are looking for a convenient way to raise money so that they can hire more employees, build more factories or offices, and upgrade their equipment. The way they raise money is by issuing shares of stock in their corporation. On the other side, you have people like you and me who buy shares of stock in these corporations. The place where we all meet, the buyers and sellers, is the stock market.

What Is a Share of Stock?

We're not talking about livestock! Actually, the word *stock* originally did come from the word *livestock*. Instead of trading cows and sheep, however, we trade pieces of paper that represent ownership—shares—in a corporation. You may also hear people refer to stocks as *equities* or *securities*. Most people just call them stocks, which means *supply*. (After all, the entire stock market is based on the economic theory of supply and demand.)

When you buy shares of stock in a corporation, you are commonly referred to as an *investor* or a *shareholder*. When you own a share of stock, you are sharing in the success of the business, and you actually become a part owner of the corporation. When you buy a stock, you get one vote for each share of stock you own. The more shares you own, therefore, the more of the corporation you control. Most shareholders own a tiny sliver of the corporation, with little control over how the corporation is run and no ability to boss anyone in the corporation around. You'd have to own millions of shares of stock to become a primary owner of a corporation whose stock is publicly traded.

In summary, a corporation issues shares of stock so that it can *attract* money. Investors are willing to buy stock in a corporation in order to receive the opportunity to sell the stock at a higher price. If the corporation does well, the stock you own will probably go up in price, and you'll make money. If the corporation does poorly, the stock you own will probably go down in price, and you'll lose money (if you sell, that is).

Stock Certificates: Fancy-Looking Pieces of Paper

Stock certificates are written proof that you have invested in the corporation. (Some people don't realize that you invest in companies, not stocks.) Although some people ask for the stock certificates so that they can keep them in a safe place, most people let a brokerage firm hold their stock certificates. It is a lot easier that way. To be technical, there are actually two kinds of stock, *common* and *preferred*. In this book, we will always be talking about common stock, because that is the only type that most corporations issue to investors. Remember, not all companies issue stock. A company has to be what is called a *corporation*, a legally defined term. Most of the large companies you have heard of are corporations, and, yes, their stocks are all traded in the stock market. I'm talking about corporations like Microsoft, IBM, Disney, General Motors, General Electric, and McDonald's.

You Buy Stocks for Only One Reason: To Make Money

The stock market is all about making money. Quite simply, if you buy stock in a corporation that is doing well and making profits, then the stock you own should go up in price. (By the way, the profits you make from a stock are called *capital gains,* which are the difference between what you paid for a stock and what you sold it for. If you lose money, it is called a *capital loss.*)

You make money in the stock market by buying a stock at one price and selling it at a higher price. It's that simple. There is no guarantee, of course, that you'll make money. Even the stocks of good corporations can sometimes go down. If you buy stocks in corporations that do well, you should be rewarded with a higher stock price. It doesn't always work out that way, but that is the risk you take when you participate in the market.

New York: Where Stock Investing Became Popular

Before there was a place called the stock market, buyers and sellers had to meet in the street. Sometime around 1790, they met every weekday under a buttonwood tree in New York. It just happened that the name of the street where all this took place was Wall Street. (For history buffs, the buttonwood tree was at 68 Wall Street.)

A lot of people heard what was happening on Wall Street and

wanted a piece of the action. On some days, as many as 100 shares of stock were exchanged! (In case you don't think that's funny, in today's market, billions of shares of stock are exchanged every day.)

It got so crowded in the early days that 24 brokers and merchants who controlled the trading activities decided to organize what they were doing. For a fixed *commission,* they agreed to buy and sell shares of stock in corporations to the public. They gave themselves a quarter for each share of stock they traded (today we would call them stockbrokers). The Buttonwood Agreement, as it was called, was signed in 1792. This was the humble beginning of the New York Stock Exchange (NYSE).

It wasn't long before the brokers and merchants moved their offices to a Wall Street coffee shop. Eventually, they moved indoors permanently to the New York Stock Exchange Building on Wall Street. Keep in mind that a stock exchange is simply a place where people go to buy and sell stocks. It provides an organized marketplace for stocks, just as a supermarket provides a marketplace for food.

Even after 200 years, the name *Wall Street* is a symbol for the U.S. stock exchanges and the financial institutions that do business with them, no matter what their physical location. If you go to New York, you'll see that Wall Street is just a narrow street in the financial district of Lower Manhattan. Therefore, the stock market, or Wall Street, is really a convenient way of talking about anyone or anything connected to our financial markets.

Three Major Stock Exchanges

After the NYSE was formed, there were also brokers trading stocks who weren't considered good enough for the New York Stock Exchange. Traders who couldn't make it on the NYSE traded on the street curb, which is why they were called curbside traders. Eventually, these traders moved indoors and established what later became the American Stock Exchange (AMEX).

There is also a third major stock exchange, the National Association of Securities Dealers Automated Quotation System (Nasdaq), which was created in 1971. This was the first electronic stock exchange; it was hooked together by a network of computers. (Yes, they did have computers back then.)

Competition is good for the stock market. It forces the stock exchanges to fill your orders faster and more cheaply. After all, they want your business. There are stock exchanges in nearly every country in the world, although the U.S. market is the largest. U.S. stock exchanges other than the three major ones include the Cincinnati Stock Exchange, the Pacific Stock Exchange, the Boston Stock Exchange, and the Philadelphia Stock Exchange (the Philadelphia Stock Exchange is our country's oldest organized stock exchange). Other countries with stock exchanges include England, Germany, Switzerland, France, Holland, Russia, Japan, China, Sweden, Italy, Brazil, Mexico, Canada, and Australia, to name only a few.

A few years ago, in order to compete more effectively against the NYSE, the National Association of Securities Dealers (NASD), which owns the Nasdaq, and the AMEX merged. Although the two exchanges are operated separately, the merger allowed them to jointly introduce new investment products. This is interesting, but it doesn't really affect you as an investor. In the end, it doesn't really matter from which exchange you buy stocks.

Joining a Stock Exchange

It's not easy for a corporation to be listed on, or join, a stock exchange because each exchange has many rules and regulations. It can take years for a corporation to meet all the requirements and join the exchange. The stock exchanges list corporations that fit the goals and philosophy of the particular exchange.

For example, the companies that are listed on the NYSE are some of the best-known and biggest corporations in the United States—blue-chip corporations like Wal-Mart, Procter & Gamble, Johnson & Johnson, and Coca-Cola. The Nasdaq, on the other hand, contains many technology corporations like Cisco Systems, Intel, and Sun Microsystems. In addition, stocks that are traded "over the counter" (OTC) are located on the

Nasdaq. By the way, there are over 5000 stocks traded on the three U.S. stock exchanges and another 5000 smaller companies traded over the counter.

Corporations: Convincing People to Buy Their Stock

Once a corporation goes public and allows its stock to be traded, the trick is to convince investors that the corporation will be profitable. Corporations do everything in their power to attract money from investors. Bigger corporations spread the word through print and television advertising. Smaller corporations might rely on word of mouth, emails, or news releases. The more people there are who believe in a corporation, the more people there will be who will buy its stock, and the more money the people on Wall Street will make. Now do you understand why everyone is always saying such good things about the market? If you're lucky, you'll also make a few bucks if you invest in a profitable corporation.

Now that you have some idea of what happens in the back rooms of the stock brokerage, I'm going to take you upstairs. First, I will introduce you to the three types of people who participate in the market: individual investors, traders, and professionals. By the time you finish this book, you should have a better idea of where you fit in.

Individual Investors

Investors buy stocks in corporations that they believe in and plan to hold those stocks for the long term (usually a year or longer). Investors generally choose to ignore the short-term day-to-day price fluctuations of the market. If all goes according to plan, they find that the value of their investment has increased over time.

One of the most profitable buy-and-hold investors of our time, Warren Buffett, likes to say that he is not buying a stock, he is buying a business. He buys stocks for the best price he can and holds them as long as he can—forever, if possible. (When asked when he sells, Buffett once said, "Never.")

Keep in mind, however, that Buffett buys stocks in conservative (some would say boring) corporations like insurance companies and banks and rarely buys technology stocks. Buffett became a billionaire using his long-term buy-and-hold investment *strategy* (a strategy is a plan that helps you determine what stocks to buy or sell).

Investors who bought shares of stock in Caterpillar (CAT), Lockheed Martin (LMT), and Minnesota Mining and Manufacturing (MMM), for example, saw the value of their investments increase over time, especially during the latter half of the 1990s. Actually, there was never a better time to be an investor than during the 1990s. You bought shares of a corporation you knew and believed in, then sat back and watched the value of the shares increase by 25, 50, or 100 percent. (This is as good as it gets for investors!)

Short-Term Traders

Unlike investors, *short-term traders* don't care about the long-term prospects of a corporation. Their goal is to take advantage of the short-term movements in a stock or the market. This means that they may buy and then sell a stock within 5 minutes, a few hours, a few days, or even a week or month on occasion. When you are a trader, you are primarily focused on the price of a stock, not on the business of the corporation.

There are many kinds of short-term traders. Some of you may have heard the term *day trader,* which refers to a very aggressive short-term trader. For example, a day trader might buy a stock at $10 a share with a plan to sell it at $10.50 or $11, usually within the same day. If the stock goes down in price, he or she will probably sell it quickly for a small loss. In other words, day traders buy stocks in the morning and sell them for a higher price a few minutes or hours later. Generally, they move all their money back to cash by the end of the day. Keep in mind that it's extremely hard to consistently make money as a day trader. Only a small percentage of people make a living at it.

Professional Traders

Professional traders use other people's money (and sometimes their own) to make investments or trades on behalf of clients. Professionals include individuals who work for Wall Street brokerages and stock exchanges, but they also include institutional traders like pension funds, banks, and mutual fund companies.

There is no doubt that institutional investors that have access to millions of dollars influence not only individual stocks but the entire market. Some of these institutions have set up computer programs that automatically buy or sell stocks when certain prices have been reached. (On days when the market is up or down hundreds of points, the stock exchanges limit how much institutional investors can buy or sell.)

If you want to be a professional Wall Street trader, you can also apply to become a member of one of the exchanges. At current prices, it will cost you several million dollars to buy a seat on the NYSE, and all you get for this is the freedom to trade stocks directly on the exchange floor. (For that kind of money, you'd think they'd let you play golf and swim! For a few million dollars less, you can trade directly from the comfort of your own home.) Some people with seats rent them out to professional traders and thus bring in extra income.

How Wall Street Keeps Score

Wall Street has several ways to keep track of the market. One of the easiest ways to find out how the market is performing each day is to look at a newspaper, television, or the Internet. Typically, people look at the Dow Jones Industrial Average (DJIA), the most popular method of determining whether the market is up or down for the day.

The Dow Jones Industrial Average

In 1884, a reporter named Charles Dow calculated an average of the closing prices of 12 railroad stocks; this became known as the Dow

Jones Transportation Average. His goal was to find a way to measure how the stock market did each day. He then wrote comments about the stock market in a four-page daily newspaper called a "flimsie," which later became the *Wall Street Journal.*

A few years later, the company Charles Dow helped start, Dow Jones, launched the Dow Jones Industrial Average, consisting of 12 industrial stocks. If you know about averages, you know that you basically add up the prices of the stocks in the index and divide by the number of stocks to create a daily average. By watching the Dow, you can get a general idea of how the market is doing. It also gives us clues to the *trend* of the market, whether it is going up, down, or sideways. (The trend is simply the direction in which a stock or market is going.)

The original 12 stocks in the Dow were the biggest and most popular companies at the end of the nineteenth century—for example, American Tobacco, Distilling and Cattle Feeding, U.S. Leather, and General Electric, to name a few. Guess which stock still remains in the index? (If you guessed General Electric, you are right. The other corporations either went out of business or merged with other corporations.)

By 1928, the Dow Jones Industrial Average was increased to 30 stocks, which is the number of stocks in the index today. (By the way, this index is sometimes called the Dow 30.) These 30 stocks are a cross section of the most important *sectors* in the stock market. (A sector is a group of companies in the same industry, such as technology, utilities, or energy.) Over time, the Dow changed from an equal-weighted index to one in which different stocks have different weights. This means that stocks with a higher weighting affect the Dow index more than stocks with a lower weighting. For example, since American Express is weighted high in today's market, if this stock is having a bad day and falls by several points, the Dow could end up down for the day.

It's easy to find out how the Dow did each day—it's reported in the media. Since more than half of the public is invested in the stock market, there is a lot of interest in what the Dow does each day.

Therefore, when we talk about the Dow Jones being up or down each day, we're really talking about a representative group of 30 stocks, the Dow 30. Even if the market is down for the day, the stock you own could be up, or the other way around.

Other Indexes

Although the Dow (operated by the *Wall Street Journal*) was the first index to keep track of stocks, hundreds of other indexes have been created to track almost everything from transportation to utilities to technology stocks. Some sophisticated investors keep an eye on many of these indexes, but most people watch just three.

The next most popular index (after the Dow) is the Nasdaq Composite Index, which tracks the more than 5000 stocks listed on the Nasdaq. On television or on the Internet, when you see the Dow listed, you will almost always see the Nasdaq below it.

The third index that many people watch closely is the S&P 500. If you guessed that this contains 500 stocks, you are right. These are 500 stocks that Standard & Poor's Corporation (S&P) has selected to represent the overall stock market. They are usually the largest stocks and include a lot of technology stocks. Other popular indexes are the Russell 2000 index and the Wilshire 5000. You'll learn later that you can invest directly in them, since they trade just like stocks.

If you were a professional money manager, your goal each year would be to beat the major indexes. What does this mean? It means that if the Dow is up 15 percent this year, you would try to get 15 percent or more. The bad news is that it's very hard for people, even professional investors, to beat the indexes. In 2001, it was reported that 50 percent of the professional money managers don't beat the indexes each year. In 2002, it was reported that only 37 percent of the professional managers beat the indexes.

It's All About Points

To measure how much you make or lose in the stock market, Wall Street uses a system of points that represent dollars. For example, if your stock went from $5 a share to $10 a share, we would say that your stock went up 5 points. That's how we keep score on Wall Street, but accountants and market analysts make it seem a lot more complicated than it is.

The same type of scoring is done with the major indexes like the Dow, the Nasdaq, and the S&P 500. If the Dow went from 10,000 to

10,100, you would say the market went up by 100 points. If your stock went from $10 a share to $11 a share, you made a point, not a dollar.

Note: Although it's okay to tell people how many points you made or your percentage gain, it's not polite to tell people the exact amount of money you made on a stock deal. Even if you made $5000 in 5 minutes, it's best to keep it to yourself. To be polite, stick to the point system and avoid talking about money.

How Much Is It Going to Cost?

If you can figure out the following calculation, then you will understand how to buy or sell stock. Just as in an auction, every stock has a price. This price changes frequently—every few seconds for some stocks. Let's say that a stock you're interested in, Bright Light, is currently trading at $20 a share. You decide you want to buy 100 shares. The math goes like this: 100 shares multiplied by $20 a share will cost you $2000. That means you must pay $2000 if you want to buy 100 shares of Bright Light (plus commission, of course).

This is so important that I'll give you another example. Let's say you want to buy 1000 shares of a stock that is selling for $15 a share. How much will it cost you? The answer is $15,000. One more example: Let's say you want to buy 100 shares of a stock that costs $5 a share. The answer is $500.

How Much Did You Make?

Let's say you decide to buy 1000 shares of a stock that costs $15 a share. It will cost you $15,000. If the stock goes to $16, you have made 1 point. If the stock goes to $17, you have made 2 points. Here's the important part: If you have 1000 shares of a stock and you made 1 point, you made $1000 in profit. If the stock goes up 2 points, you made $2000 in profit. So the more shares you own, the more money you'll make (or lose).

(More examples? If you own 100 shares of a stock and it goes up 1 point, you made $100. If you own 100 shares of a stock and it goes up by 5 points, you made $500.)

What If No One Wants to Buy or Sell Your Stock?

This is actually a very good question. It's like having a house sale that no one goes to. To solve this problem, the stock exchanges have set up a system in which there is always someone on the other side of a transaction. In other words, there will always be a buyer or seller for you. You may not get the best price, but at least you know that there is someone who is willing to sell you the stock or buy it from you if you own it.

On the NYSE, there is one person, a *specialist,* who acts as the intermediary for each stock. The specialists "make a market" for every stock listed on the exchange. This means that the specialist keeps track of and fills all of the orders for a particular stock that comes in, sometimes using his or her own money if no one else wants to buy or sell the stock. Does this sound like a fun job? Handheld computers make the job a lot easier. Before computers, the specialists used to fill the orders by hand. Once orders increased from hundreds to billions of shares, computers were installed to handle the orders.

You might wonder how the specialists get paid, since they are using their own money to fill the orders. First of all, because specialists know the stock so well, they are able to buy it at the lowest possible price and sell it to you at the highest possible price. It doesn't sound really fair, but that's how they make their money. They also get a cut on every trade they make. They claim this is to compensate them for the risk they take when they use their own money to buy or sell.

If you are investing in only a few hundred shares, or even a few thousand, it's not worth your time to worry too much about the pennies the intermediaries make on each trade. It's the million-share traders who try to save money on each trade. By the way, those pennies add up to thousands of dollars every day for the specialists. They make money whether the market goes up or down.

At the Nasdaq market, the computerized stock exchange, buyers and sellers are matched with the help of an intermediary called a *market maker.* Unlike the arrangement at the NYSE, where only one specialist is assigned to a stock, at the Nasdaq you can have multiple market makers for a stock. The more popular the stock, the more market makers will be assigned to the stock.

For instance, a stock like Microsoft could have as many as 30 market makers, while a $1 stock might have only one market maker. There is, however, at least one market maker assigned to each Nasdaq stock. Keep in mind that all of this happens behind the scenes within seconds. Because billions of shares are traded each day, your orders end up being routed by computers. It is nice to know, however, that there will always be someone who is willing to buy or sell shares of your stock.

Why Stocks Are a Good Idea

There are a number of reasons why you should buy stocks. According to researchers, stocks have beaten every other type of investment over any 10-year period during the last 75 years. They are a good buy even after a market crash or an extended bear market. According to research conducted by Jeremy Siegel, best-selling author of *Stocks for the Long Run* (McGraw-Hill, 2002), over the long term stocks gained an annualized 8 percent after inflation after the market has fallen by over 40 percent or more. (*Inflation* is the expansion of the money supply. As a result, the price of goods and services go up, which lowers or erodes the amount you can buy with your money.) In the short term, stocks are riskier than fixed-income assets, but in the long run, says Siegel, stocks outperform every other investment.

According to many experts, stocks have returned an average of 11 percent annually for the last 75 years, handily beating inflation as well as bonds, money market accounts, and savings accounts. In addition, it's cheaper to buy stocks over the long term, especially if you buy and hold. And according to the experts, the odds are quite good that the market will continue to go up just as it's done in the past (although there are no guarantees).

Risk: The Chance You Take When You Buy Stocks

A lot of people enter the stock market without a clear idea of the risks. (Too many people look up at the stars without looking out for the rocks below.) Let's be clear: when you invest or trade in the market, there is a

chance that you could lose some or all of your money. It's even possible
to lose more money than you put in. The goal for many investors and
traders, therefore, is learning how to recognize and minimize risk. Keep
in mind, however, that you can't completely eliminate risk, but you can
learn to manage it.

There are all kinds of risk. First, the entire stock market could go
down in price because of outside events like war, recession, or terrorism.
Second, even if the stock market as a whole goes up, there are a number
of reasons why your stock could go down. Third, even if you avoid the
stock market and put your money in a savings account (or under your
mattress), there is the risk that your money will be worth less because of
inflation. And finally, if you do not invest in the market, there is the risk
that you will miss out on some very profitable buying opportunities.
Therefore, whether you invest in the market or not, there will be risks.
By the time you finish this book, you'll be able to decide for yourself
whether the risks you take are worth the rewards you'll make.

The Dow 30 (including ticket symbol)

Alcoa (AA)
American Express Co. (AXP)
AT&T Corp. (T)
Boeing Co. (BA)
Caterpillar, Inc. (CAT)
Citigroup, Inc. (C)
Coca-Cola Co. (KO)
DuPont Co. (DD)
Eastman Kodak Co. (EK)
ExxonMobil Corp. (XOM)
General Electric Co. (GE)
General Motors Corp. (GM)
Hewlett-Packard Co. (HPQ)
Home Depot (HD)
Honeywell International Inc. (HON)
Intel Corp. (INTC)
International Business Machines Corp. (IBM)
International Paper Co. (IP)
J.P. Morgan Chase (JPM)
Johnson & Johnson (JNJ)

McDonald's Corp. (MCD)
Merck & Co. (MRK)
Microsoft (MSFT)
Minnesota Mining and Manufacturing Co. (MMM)
Philip Morris and Co. (MO)
Procter & Gamble Co. (PG)
SBC Communications (SBC)
United Technologies Corp. (UTX)
Wal-Mart Stores, Inc. (WMT)
Walt Disney Co. (DIS)

In the next chapter, you will learn how to invest in bonds, cash, mutual funds, and real estate.

2

Stocks: Not Your Only Investment

When most people talk about the stock market, they are usually referring to buying or selling individual stocks. There are, however, a number of other investments besides stocks. Becoming familiar with other types of investments—for example, *bonds,* cash, real estate, and *mutual funds*—will help make you a more knowledgeable investor.

Bonds: Misunderstood but Popular Fixed-Income Investments

Wall Street helps corporations raise money not only by issuing stocks, but also by issuing bonds. Technically, a bond is a fixed-income investment issued by a corporation or the government that gives you a regular or fixed rate of interest for a specific period.

To understand bonds, you have to think like a lender, not an investor. After all, a bond is an IOU. When you buy bonds, you are lending money to the corporation or the government in return for a promise that the money will be paid back in full with interest.

In "bondspeak," the corporation or government promises to pay you a fixed rate of interest, let's say 7 percent per year. The fixed rate of interest is called a *coupon*. You are guaranteed to receive this fixed interest rate for the length of the loan. At the end of the period (called the *maturity date*), you are given your original money back, and you get to keep all the interest you made on the loan.

There are three types of bonds: *Treasuries, munis,* and *corporate*. Bonds issued by the U.S. government are called Treasuries. They are considered the safest bond investment because they have the full backing of the U.S. government. Munis are issued by state and local governments and are usually tax-free. Corporate bonds have the most risk but also provide the highest returns.

There are three categories of bonds: bills, notes, and bonds. Bills have the shortest maturity dates, from 1 to 12 months; notes have maturity dates ranging from 1 to 10 years; and bonds have maturity dates of 10 years or longer, often as long as 30 years. Usually, the longer the term of the loan, the higher the *yield* will be. (The yield is what you will actually earn from the bond.)

Bonds can be confusing so I'll give several examples: Let's say you decide to lend a corporation $5000 for 10 years. In return, the corporation pays you 10 percent a year. That means that for the next 10 years you'll receive $500 a year in interest payments. To review, the bond has a $5000 face value (how much it costs), a 10 percent coupon (a fixed interest rate), and a 10-year maturity (time period). That wasn't hard, was it?

Usually, people who don't like a lot of risk tend to buy bonds rather than stocks. With stocks, there is the chance you could lose all your money if the stock goes to zero. Unfortunately, bonds aren't perfect either. In fact, there are risks in buying bonds.

For example, there is always the chance that the corporation you lent money to will go bankrupt. This is what happened to the bondholders of Enron, WorldCom, Global Crossing, and other corporations. When you buy a bond, it is given a rating (highly rated AAA bonds are considered the safest). The lower the bond rating, however, the higher the interest you receive. Some bonds are so risky that they are called *junk bonds*. For the risk you take when you own lower-rated bonds, you receive an extremely high yield.

Bondholders are very concerned about interest rates. After all, many bondholders live off the interest payments they receive from their bonds. After the market peaked in 2000, the Federal Reserve System (the Fed) lowered interest rates more than 12 times. Existing bondholders were delighted because they had already locked in a favorable yield at a higher interest rate and could resell their bonds for a higher price. After all, when interest rates fall, the value of the bond goes up.

The inverse relationship between bond prices and interest rates can be confusing. Many people don't realize that the price you received when your bond was issued rises or falls in the opposite direction with interest rates (the inverse relationship). For example, let's say you purchased a bond for $1000 with an 8 percent coupon (it pays $80 annually per $1000 of face value). If interest rates drop below 8 percent, your bond will be worth more than $1000 because investors will pay more to receive the higher interest rate on your bond. On the other hand, if interest rates rise, your bond will be worth less than $1000 because buyers won't pay you face value for a bond that pays a lower interest rate.

To summarize, the advantage of owning bonds is that you receive a guaranteed interest payment and a promise that your original money (called *principal*) will be repaid to you in full. Basically, you lend money to a corporation, and it promises to pay you back in full after a specified period of time. The disadvantage is that the corporation could go out of business, leaving you with nothing. You may be surprised to learn that more people buy bonds than invest in the stock market. Bonds are especially popular with people who are nearing retirement.

If bonds seem confusing, don't worry; they are. That is why many people prefer to buy bond mutual funds, which are more convenient and easier to understand. Speaking of mutual funds, it's about time we learned more about this fascinating investment. It fits in perfectly with our discussion about the stock market.

Mutual Funds: A Popular Alternative to Individual Stocks and Bonds

Instead of investing directly in the stock market, you can buy *mutual funds.* An investment company creates a mutual fund by pooling investors' money and using it to invest in an assortment of stocks, bonds, or cash. In a way, investing in a mutual fund is like hiring your own professional money manager. The best part is that the fund manager who manages the mutual fund makes the buying and selling decisions for you. This is ideal for people who don't have the time or knowledge to research individual companies and determine whether the stock is a good buy at its current price. This is one of the reasons that mutual funds have become so popular in the last few years.

For a relatively low fee, especially when compared with stock commissions, mutual funds give you instant *diversification.* For a minimum investment of $2500, or sometimes less, you can buy a slice of a whole basket of stocks. (Many mutual fund companies have raised their minimum from as little as $100 to $2500.) If you are interested in mutual funds, you should begin by looking in the financial section of your local newspaper. There are well over 7000 mutual funds to choose from, each with its own style and strategy.

For example, you could buy a mutual fund that invests in stocks (called a stock fund), technology (a sector fund), or bonds (a bond fund), or one that invests in international stocks (an international fund). No matter what kind of investment you're interested in, there is a mutual fund that should meet your needs.

When you find a mutual fund that meets your goals and fits your investment strategy, you send a check to the investment company. Because there are so many mutual funds, you should take as much time to choose the correct mutual fund as you would take to choose a stock. Keep in mind that although most mutual funds did extremely well during the 1990s, many have faltered during the last few years. That's why it's important to find a fund that is successful even when the economy is doing poorly.

One of the smartest ways to invest in mutual funds is through a 401(k), a voluntary tax-deferred savings plan that is provided by a number of companies. The popular 401(k) plan is one of the reasons so many people became involved in the stock market to begin with. The brilliant part of the 401(k) is that you don't have to pay taxes on the money you earn until you are 59½. If you leave the company before you're 59½, you can convert your 401(k) to an IRA, another type of tax-deferred savings plan. IRA rules are complex, so seek professional tax advice.

Why People Choose Mutual Funds

The main reason that people choose mutual funds is to allow diversification, which means that instead of investing all of your money in only one stock—a frequently risky move—you are able to buy a slice of hundreds of stocks. For example, let's say that most of your money was invested in WorldCom on the day it announced that it had misstated its earnings by $3.8 billion. The stock fell by over 90 percent in 1 day! If you had owned this stock directly, you would have lost 90 percent of your money. On the other hand, if you owned a mutual fund that owned WorldCom, you might have lost no more than 3 percent of your money that day. Now do you see why mutual funds are a good idea for investors?

On the other hand, some people are looking for a whole lot more, which is what brings them to the stock market in the first place. If you owned a mutual fund that contained a stock that went up a lot in price in 1 day, you might make 1 or 2 percent on your fund that day. But if you owned the stock directly, you could make 10 or 20 percent, or perhaps more, in 1 or 2 days. (I've owned stocks that have gone up as much as 50 percent in 1 day.)

Net Asset Value

A net asset value (NAV) is similar to a stock price. It technically refers to the value of one share in the mutual fund. You can find NAVs in the financial section of your daily newspaper. The math is very similar to that for a stock. If you want to buy 100 shares of a mutual fund with an NAV of $10, it will cost you $1000. You'll also be charged a very small management fee, which is simply subtracted from the NAV.

You can also look in the newspaper to see how well your mutual fund did during various periods, from yesterday to 3 years ago. The mutual fund corporations have done an excellent job of letting their shareholders know exactly what their performance records are. If you don't like a fund's investment performance, you can always switch to another mutual fund.

If you have never invested in the stock market, you might seriously consider getting your feet wet with mutual funds. You should know that there are two types of funds: *no-load* and *load*. In my opinion, you are better off with a no-load fund (which means that you won't have to pay extra sales charges for investing in the fund) because it's cheaper. There is no evidence that load funds are any better than no-load funds.

The highly regulated mutual fund industry has avoided scandal until recently. Some funds allowed professional investors such as hedge funds to trade after hours or market time. New, stricter rules should help to reduce unfair practices.

Mutual funds aren't perfect, of course. Sometimes they go down, almost as much as stocks. During the recent bear market, many mutual funds went down a lot (a few lost as much as 70 percent)—not all mutual funds, but many of them. Most mutual funds are designed to do well in bull markets and tend to fail miserably during bear markets (although a handful of specialized mutual funds shine in bear markets).

Index Funds: A Popular Alternative to Actively Managed Mutual Funds

The mutual funds I've talked about so far are run by fund managers who keep close tabs on how their funds are doing. They will buy or sell stocks in order to make more money for the fund. These fund managers are actively involved in improving the performance of their mutual fund; that's why they're called active managers.

Index funds are run differently. Like other mutual funds, they use money pooled by investors. But unlike other mutual funds, index funds do not have active managers. They simply contain the stocks that make up one of the various indexes. For example, you could buy the Dow 30 index (DIA), the S&P 500 index (SPY), or the Nasdaq 100 index (QQQQ). The idea is that if you can't beat the indexes, you might as well join them. Therefore, if the Dow index is having a good year and is up 10 percent, you will get a 10 percent return on your fund.

Index funds are less expensive than other mutual funds because you don't have to pay an active manager and there are no extra sales charges. For these reasons, index funds have become very popular with the public. More than 50 percent of portfolio managers have failed to beat the index funds (in some years, the records are even worse), and so index funds are a popular alternative.

Keep in mind that in a bull market, index funds do well. During a lengthy bear market, however, their performance will be terrible. (Bull markets are markets in which the major stock indexes are consistently going up because investors are buying stocks. On the other hand, bear markets are markets in which the major stock indexes are consistently going down because investors are avoiding or selling stocks.) Nevertheless, the low cost and high performance of index funds have made them attractive to many investors.

Cash

During the 1990s, putting your money in cash or a *certificate of deposit* (CD) seemed like a dumb idea. After all, a CD, offered by most banks and financial institutions, gave you a return of no more than 5 percent a year. At the time, people became giddy when they saw the value of their stocks go up by huge amounts. A 5 percent return on a CD seemed like a bad joke.

The joke backfired, however, when people held their favorite stocks too long. By the year 2001, the market had reversed. Many investors who had held onto their favorite stocks lost nearly everything. Those 5 percent CDs and an old-fashioned savings account (paying only 1 percent a year) seemed like mighty good ideas. One percent a year isn't much—in fact, it's a terrible return—but it's better than losing money.

If you have a preference for cash, you can also put your money in a *money market fund,* which pays a little more than a bank. (A money market fund is a mutual fund that invests in such short-term securities as CDs and *commercial paper.*) You can also invest directly in U.S. Treasury bills, which offer the advantage of safety because they have the backing of the U.S. government. (Money market funds aren't insured.)

Remember when I talked about diversification? By keeping some of your excess cash in a money market account, you are protected from vicious bear markets. In addition, you can use excess cash to buy your favorite stock or mutual fund. You'll also learn that it's nice to have extra cash on the side to pay for emergencies and unexpected expenses. There's no rule that says that every cent you have should be invested in the stock market.

Investing in Real Estate and Real Estate Investment Trusts (REITs)

One of the smartest investments you can make is to buy your own home. Not only will you get tax breaks, but over the years the prices of many homes have skyrocketed. (In some parts of the country, the price of real estate has gone up so high that it reminds people of what happened to the stock market after it peaked in 2000.) Owning a home is usually cheaper than renting, it allows you to build long-term wealth the old-fashioned way, and, most important, it feels great to be a homeowner.

The biggest negative of owning a home is that real estate is an illiquid investment (meaning that you can't sell it quickly, as you can a stock or mutual fund). The other downside is that you are required to make monthly mortgage payments. If for some reason you fall behind with your payments, the bank can attempt to take over your home. Also, when you own a home, you have to pay property taxes, homeowner's insurance, and interest on the loan. Even with these drawbacks, owning a home is a worthy financial goal, although it's not for everyone. (For example, renting is simpler and more convenient for some people. In addition, you could use the money you aren't spending on the house to invest in the stock market.)

Many people use real estate as an investment. This includes buying a residential property, such as a single-family home, condominium, or townhouse. If all goes according to plan, you can turn around and sell it for a higher price or rent it out. As with investing in the stock market, you never want to buy real estate until you have done extensive research.

An alternative to buying real estate is to invest in a REIT, a publicly traded company whose stock can be bought and sold on one of the stock exchanges. These companies purchase and manage various real estate properties. If you don't want to take the time to buy stocks in these companies, you can always buy REIT mutual funds.

Unlike real estate, the main advantage of REITs is their liquidity. In addition, you can enjoy the benefits of buying and selling real estate without having to do the work. Of course, there is the risk that the company or fund manager will make poor real estate investments, causing the REIT to go down in price.

Bull, Bear, and Sideways Markets

Bear Market

Sometimes the market goes through a period of months or even years when it keeps going down. That has happened a number of times in the history of the stock market. When the stock market is officially in a bear market, it means that the major market indexes—the Dow, Nasdaq, and S&P 500—are declining. People sell their stocks for whatever price they can get. In general, the economy is weak, and corporate earnings are declining.

A bear market is pretty depressing for Wall Street. People begin to avoid the stock market and put their money in cash, gold, or bonds. On Wall Street, the major brokerages stop hiring or lay off employees. Since the stock market often predicts what will happen to the economy, a lengthy bear market may signal that a recession is coming. No one can predict how long a bear market will last, although bear markets in the past have been relatively short.

Bull Market

Bull markets are very profitable for most traders and investors. During a bull market, there are plenty of jobs on Wall Street, and investors are flush with cash that they eagerly use to buy more stocks. Everyone seems to be in a stock buying mood, and the major indexes have nowhere to go but up. People are optimistic about the direction of the country. Everyone is talking about how much money they made in the market. In the early 1920s, the bull market was fueled by the increased use of automobiles and electricity. In the great bull market of the 1990s, it was the Internet that drove stock prices higher.

Sideways Market

Wall Street dreads a sideways market because it's hard for anyone to make money in such a market. In a sideways market, the market indexes attempt to go up or down but end up just about where they started. People just sit on the sidelines, holding their cash and refusing to participate in the market. For example, the market reached its low 3 years after the 1929 market crash, then went nowhere for the next 10 years. It took another 12 years for the market to return to its 1929 highs. Another sideways market began in 1966, when the Dow was at 983.51. You had to wait 16 years, until 1982, for the Dow to permanently break 1000 (although it temporarily broke through in 1972 before retreating.) Investors had to endure a number of mini-bear markets during this period.

In the next chapter, you will learn about growth, income, and value stocks, and introduced to penny stocks.

How to
Classify Stocks

If you want to understand the stock market, you should learn the different ways in which people classify and identify stocks.

Stock Sectors

A *sector* is a group of companies that loosely belong to the same industry and provide the same product or service. Examples of stock sectors include airlines, software, chemicals, oil, retail, automobiles, and pharmaceuticals, to name just a few. Understanding sectors is important if you want to make money in the stock market. The reason is simple: No matter how the market is doing and no matter what the condition of the economy, there are always sectors that are doing well and sectors that are struggling.

For example, during the recent bear market, the semiconductor sector, the Internet sector, and the computer sector were going down on a regular basis. A lot of savvy investors shifted their money out of these losing sectors and moved into the retail and housing sectors. That's right, the retail and housing sectors soared during 2001 and 2002. (Wal-Mart was particularly strong.)

Some professional traders shift their money into and out of sectors every day. Once they identify the strongest sectors for the day, they pick what they think is the most profitable stock in each of these sectors. Like anything connected to the stock market, shifting into and out of sectors sounds easier on paper than it is in real life. It's always easier to look in the rearview mirror to figure out what sectors were most profitable.

It's very easy for me to say that you should have shifted out of technology in March 2000 and moved into the housing sector. But now, right now, how confident are you that housing stocks will continue to go up in price? It's a lot harder to pick successful sectors than many people think. Nevertheless, it's worth taking the time to understand and identify the various sectors and to be aware of which sectors are strong and which are weak. This could give you a clue as to where the economy is headed.

Classifying Stocks: Income, Value, and Growth

Income Stocks

The first category of stocks is *income stocks,* which include shares of corporations that give money back to shareholders in the form of *dividends* (some people call these stocks *dividend stocks*). Some investors, usually older individuals who are near retirement, are attracted to income stocks because they live off the income in the form of dividends and interest on the stocks and bonds they own. In addition, stocks that pay a regular dividend are less volatile. They may not rise or fall as quickly as other stocks, which is fine with the conservative investors who tend to buy income stocks. Another advantage of stocks that pay dividends is that the dividends reduce the loss if the stock price goes down.

There are also a number of disadvantages of buying income stocks. First, dividends are considered taxable income, so you have to report the money you receive to the IRS. Second, if the company doesn't raise its dividend each year—and many don't—inflation can cut into your profits. Finally, income stocks can fall just as quickly as other stocks. Just because you own stock in a so-called conservative company doesn't mean you will be protected if the stock market falls.

Value Stocks

Value stocks are stocks of profitable companies that are selling at a reasonable price compared with their true worth, or value. The trick, of course, is determining what a company is really worth—what investors call its *intrinsic value*. Some low-priced stocks that seem like bargains are low-priced for a reason.

Value stocks are often those of old-fashioned companies, such as insurance companies and banks, that are likely to increase in price in the future, even if not as quickly as other stocks. It takes a lot of research to find a company whose price is a bargain compared to its value. Investors who are attracted to value stocks have a number of fundamental tools (e.g., *P/E ratios*) that they use to find these bargain stocks. (I'll discuss many of these tools in Chapter 9.)

Growth Stocks

Growth stocks are the stocks of companies that consistently earn a lot of money (usually 15 percent or more per year) and are expected to grow faster than the competition. They are often in high-tech industries. The price of growth stocks can be very high even if the company's earnings aren't spectacular. This is because growth investors believe that the corporation will earn money in the future and are willing to take the risk.

Most of the time, growth stocks won't pay a dividend, as the corporation wants to use every cent it earns to improve or grow the business. Because growth stocks are so volatile, they can make sudden price moves in either direction. This is ideal for short-term traders but unnerving for many investors. During the 1990s, when growth stocks were all the rage, even buy-and-hold investors couldn't resist investing in growth companies like Cisco, Sun Microsystems, and Dell Computer.

Dividends: Another Way to Make Money

You already know that many investors are attracted to income stocks because they pay dividends. Let's take a closer look at exactly how dividends work.

As mentioned before, a corporation that has made a lot of profits passes some of those profits to shareholders in the form of a payment called a dividend. It is usually given to shareholders in cash (in fact, by check), or, if desired, it can be used to buy more shares of the stock.

Dividends are a great idea. Not only do you make money as the price of your stock goes up, but you can also receive a bonus from the corporation in the form of a dividend every quarter. Keep in mind that the corporation's board of directors is not required to distribute a dividend but often does so when the corporation is doing well.

If you own a lot of shares of a stock, perhaps 5000 shares or more, your dividend payments can add up substantially. Let's say, for example, that a corporation pays $0.25 per share quarterly dividend on your 5000 shares, which adds up to $1 in dividends each year. That means that every 3 months you will receive $1250, for a total of $5000 a year. In addition, if the stock you own goes up in price, then you also make money on the gain (assuming you sell the stock).

People used to talk a lot about dividends, especially investors who were nearing retirement age, because so many investors depended on their dividend checks to live. Some people will buy only stocks that pay hefty dividends. The corporations that traditionally paid dividends were the large blue-chip companies that are included in the Dow Jones Industrial Average (in the game of poker, blue chips are the most valuable). Corporations of these types tended to attract older investors who were more interested in the dividends than in the stock price.

Unfortunately, a lot of corporations, even the blue chips, have lowered or eliminated their dividends. In the go-go 1990s, corporations wanted to use every cent they had to enlarge or improve their business and weren't willing to give some of that money back to their shareholders. Technology corporations in particular weren't in the habit of paying dividends. You can easily find out the amount of the dividend, if any, that a corporation pays by looking in the newspaper.

Penny Stocks

Just as their name suggests, penny stocks are stocks that usually sell for less than a dollar a share (although some people define a penny stock as one selling for less than $5 a share). Because the stocks of these small corporations usually don't meet the minimum requirements for listing on a major stock exchange, they trade in the over-the-counter market (OTC) on the Nasdaq. They are also called pink sheet stocks because at one time the names and prices of these stocks were printed on pink paper. (To check the prices of unlisted OTC stocks, try the Web site www.otcbb.com.)

The advantage of trading penny stocks is that the share price is so low that almost everyone can afford to buy shares. For example, with only $1000 you can buy 2000 shares of a $0.50 penny stock. If the stock ever makes it to a dollar, you made a 100 percent profit. That is the beauty of penny stocks. On the other hand, you could put your order in at $0.75 a share, and a couple of days later the stock could fall to $0.50. It happens all the time. A number of traders specialize in these stocks, although this is not easy.

After all, penny stocks are so cheap for a reason. That reason could be poor management, no earnings, or too much debt, but whatever it is, there usually aren't enough buyers to make the stock go higher. Even with their low price, the trading *volume* on penny stocks is exceptionally low. (For example, a stock like Microsoft will trade millions of shares per day, whereas a penny stock might trade 10,000 shares, or sometimes even less.)

With a low-volume stock, it's easy for someone to manipulate the price. Manipulation? Yes, it happens, especially with penny stocks. If you have a $1 stock that is trading only 25,000 shares a day, when someone comes in to buy 10,000 shares, that trade is likely to affect the price. (That's also why some people prefer trading penny stocks.)

Because of their low volume, penny stocks are also the favorite investment of unethical people who work in *boiler rooms*. A boiler room is an operation that hires a team of people to make phone calls to people they don't know in order to convince them to buy a nearly worthless stock. As the stock price goes up (because people are urged to buy the stock), the workers (the insiders) in the boiler room sell their shares for a substantial gain. By the time you want to sell, it is often too late. More than likely, you'll lose most or all of your investment.

A bit of advice: If a cold-calling salesperson begs you to buy a penny stock, just hang up. "Hey, buddy, the stock is only $0.10 a share. For $1000, you can buy 10,000 shares. If the stock goes to a dollar, you could make $10,000. How does that sound? So can I count on you for 10,000 shares? Trust me, this stock is hot."

It is reported that thousands of people fall for this scam every single day. The boiler room brokers are skilled at making you feel that you are going to miss out on the deal of a lifetime if you don't buy in the next 10 minutes. In reality, it's unlikely that the penny stock will ever claw its way out of the basement. (An entertaining movie called *Boiler Room* described some of the tactics used to convince unsuspecting investors to buy penny stocks.)

Like anything connected to the stock market, exceptions can be found. There are a number of once high-flying companies that trade for less than a dollar. Because of these companies' history and *book value* (how much the company is worth), they are generally better buys than unknown penny stocks with no price history and negative earnings. However, it is essential that you do your homework before you purchase your first penny stock.

The SEC: Protecting Investors against Fraud

You may wonder whether there is a government organization that protects the needs and interests of the individual investor. Actually, there is. Congress created the U.S. Securities and Exchange Commission (SEC) in 1934 to regulate the securities industry after the disastrous 1929 crash. The SEC is something like the police officer for the investment industry. It sets the rules and regulations and standards that Wall Street must follow. The purpose of the SEC (paid for by your tax dollars) is to protect individual investors against fraud and to make sure the markets are run fairly and honestly. Its Web site, www.sec.gov, contains helpful articles and resources about the SEC's mission and about individual companies. It's worth mentioning that knowledge is your best weapon against fraud, and the SEC does its best to keep you informed. It will also make life miserable for anyone it catches breaking the securities laws.

Unfortunately, not everyone wants a government organization like the SEC breathing down the necks of corporations. Although Congress created the SEC, there are powerful people with special interests who want to keep the SEC as weak as possible. To make sure that the SEC is ineffective, some politicians see to it that the SEC doesn't have the funds or resources it needs to go after companies that break securities laws.

A weak SEC is nothing but an invitation to corporate crooks to use the stock market to finance their illegal trading activities. It may take a market crash or some other financial disaster before the SEC gets the tools it needs to rid the market of crooks. As an individual investor or trader, however, it pays to know your rights (and what is allowed by law), especially if you are a victim of fraud by anyone connected with the securities industry.

In the next chapter, you will learn about all the things that people do with stocks, including other ways to classify stocks.

C H A P T E R 4

Fun Things You Can Do (with Stocks)

You can do a number of interesting things with stocks: You can diversify, allocate, compound, split them, and short them. Let's look at each of these concepts in turn.

Diversification: Avoiding Putting All of Your Eggs in One Basket

I've already mentioned the importance of diversification, meaning that instead of betting your entire *portfolio* on one or two stocks, you spread the risk by investing in a variety of securities, with the number and the specific securities depending on how much risk you want to take and how long you will stick with your investment. (A portfolio is a list of the securities, including stocks, mutual funds, bonds, and cash, that you own.) The idea behind diversification is that even if one investment goes sour, your other investments might soar.

Many people's portfolios were destroyed during the recent bear market because they invested all of their money in one stock, often that of the company for which they worked. For example, if the only stock you owned was Enron because you worked there, not only did you lose your job when Enron filed for bankruptcy, but you lost your investment as well.

Let's see how diversification works when you are 100 percent invested in the stock market. First of all, you need a lot of money to properly diversify, more than most people can afford. That's because you need to own at least 25 to 50 stocks in various industries to be properly diversified (now you understand why mutual funds are such a good idea). Many financial experts suggest that you own a mixture of growth, value, and income stocks, along with a smattering of international stocks. You might also own stocks in both large companies and smaller ones.

It takes considerable skill to determine how you should diversify because so much depends on how much risk you are comfortable with (called *risk tolerance*), your age, and your investment goals. For example, when the Internet stocks were going up, many people put 100 percent of their money into those stocks. Unfortunately, this wasn't proper diversification. Although putting all their eggs in one basket did make some people rich on paper, most of the people who did this didn't understand the risks they were taking until it was too late. (Many people thought they were properly diversified until all of their investments went down at once.)

In my opinion, if you insist on investing 100 percent of your money in stocks (and even if you add mutual funds, bonds, and cash to the mix), you should speak to a financial planner or adviser about proper diversification. There are so many possible combinations that diversifying your money can be mind-boggling. On the one hand, you don't want to play it too safe by being overdiversified. On the other hand, you don't want to expose yourself to too much risk.

Asset Allocation: Deciding How Much Money to Allot to Each Investment

Once you have diversified, you have to decide what percentage of your money you want to allocate (or distribute) to each investment. For example, if you are 30 years away from retirement, you might invest 65 percent in individual stocks and stock mutual funds and 25 percent in bonds, and keep 10 percent in cash. This is asset allocation. As with diversification, the correct asset allocation depends on your age, your risk tolerance, and when you'll need the money. In the old days, you were told to subtract your age from 100 to determine the percentage to put into stocks. Unfortunately, it's a lot more complicated than that. Once again, it is a good idea to seek professional help in determining the ideal asset allocation for yourself.

In a real-life example, one 80-year-old man I know had 90 percent of his portfolio in only two stocks, Lucent and Cisco Systems. When these stocks plummeted, his two-stock portfolio was ruined. Now he's worried that he won't have enough money to survive, and he's right. The goal for this man is to protect his original investment. On the other hand, I have a 21-year-old friend who is putting much of her money in stocks and stock mutual funds, and she can afford to do so because her time horizon is so much longer.

Compounding: Creating Earnings on Your Earnings

There is something you can do with stocks that can make you rich, according to the mathematicians who dream up this stuff. The idea behind compounding is the reason that people began to buy and hold stocks in the first place. Compounding works like this: You reinvest any money you make on your savings or investments: interest, dividends, or capital gains. The longer you keep reinvesting your earnings, the more money you'll make.

For example, if you invest $100 and it grows by 10 percent in one year, at the end of the year you'll have a total of $110. If you leave the money alone, you'll have $121 by the end of the next year. The extra $11 is called *compound earnings,* or the earnings that are earned on earnings. The more your investment is earning, the faster the compounding. The advocates of compounding remind you to invest early if you want to have more money later.

Compounding is a neat accounting maneuver that can make you rich if you live long enough to see it work. The idea is that as the stock you own goes up, it compounds in value, bringing you even greater profits. The longer you leave your money in a stock, the more it compounds over time. John Bogle, ex-chairman of the mutual fund company Vanguard, called compounding "the greatest mathematical discovery of all time for the investor seeking maximum reward."

The only problem with compounding formulas is that they make assumptions that may not occur in real life. Compounding works like a charm as long as your stock goes up in price. The problem with the stock market (and compounding) is that there are no guarantees that your stock will go up in price or that you'll make 8 percent or more a year in the market.

The Stock Split: Convincing People to Buy Your Stock

When a corporation announces a 2-for-1 stock split, this simply means that the price of the stock is cut in half but the number of shares you own is doubled. For example, let's say you own 100 shares of IBM at $80. If IBM announces a 2-for-1 stock split, the price of IBM would be cut in half, to $40 a share. Now, instead of owning 100 shares of IBM, you'd own 200 shares. From a mathematical perspective, nothing has changed at all. You own twice as many shares, but since the price of the stock is reduced by half, the value of your investment is exactly the same. (You can also have a 3-for-1 or 4-for-1 stock split.)

A stock split is often done for psychological reasons more than anything else. In this example, the price of IBM has dropped from $80 to $40 a share. Investors who are primarily focused on price might consider the $40 price a bargain, something like a half-off sale. In reality, a stock split doesn't change the corporation's financial condition at all. Instead, the biggest advantage of a stock split is that it may lure more investors—those who felt that they couldn't afford to buy IBM at $80. During the bull market, after a company announced a stock split, the stock price often went up.

Nevertheless, there are practical reasons for a company to split its stock. For example, do you know what would happen if a corporation never split its stock? Think about Berkshire Hathaway, Warren

Buffett's corporation. As I write this book, his stock is trading at $70,000 a share. That is not a typo! Most people couldn't afford even one share of stock at that price. So from a practical standpoint, stock splits do make sense for corporations. They do nothing to increase the value of the corporation, however. Splitting the stock is purely an accounting (or marketing!) procedure designed to make a stock more enticing to investors.

Some companies with low stock prices have used another type of maneuver, the *reverse split,* to artificially pump up the price of their stock so that they aren't delisted from a stock exchange. For example, if a stock is trading for $1 a share, after a 1-for-5 reverse split, the price will rise to $5 a share. Just as with the regular stock split, fundamentally nothing has changed in the company. If you are a shareholder, the value of your shares remains the same, but you now own fewer shares. (Let's say you own 100 shares of a $1 stock. After a 1-for-5 reverse split, the stock rises to $5, but the 100 shares you own are reduced to 20 shares. From an accounting standpoint, you still own $100 worth of stock.) The bad news about reverse splits is that most of the time the higher stock price doesn't last. Before long, the stock may return to $1 a share.

Selling Short: Profiting from a Falling Stock

When you invest in a stock hoping that it will rise in price, you are said to be "long" the stock. Your goal is to buy low and sell high. Your profit is the difference between the price at which you bought the stock and your selling price. On the other hand, if you hope that a stock will go down in price, you are said to be "short" the stock. When you short a stock, you first sell the stock, hoping to buy it back at a lower price. Your profit is the difference between the price at which you sold the stock and the price at which you bought it back. If you've never shorted stocks, it sounds strange until you do it a few times.

Imagine making money when a stock goes down in price! For many people, it sounds almost un-American or unethical to profit from a falling stock. In reality, you're in the market for only one reason: to make money. It doesn't matter whether you go long or short as long as you make profits. It's neither un-American nor unethical to short stocks. It's a sophisticated strategy that allows you to profit even during dismal economic conditions.

For example, let's say you are watching Bright Light, and you believe that over the next month it will go down in price. Perhaps there is negative news about the industry, or perhaps you notice that the company has a lot of debt. You decide to short 100 shares of Bright Light at the current market price of $20 a share, so you call your brokerage firm or use your online account. When you place the order, the brokerage firm will lend you 100 shares of Bright Light (since you don't own it). Let's say Bright Light falls to $18 a share. You now buy back the shares that you borrowed for a 2-point profit.

In the past, you could only short when a stock is temporarily rising, called the "uptick rule." In 2006, this controversial rule was removed, allowing short sellers to short stocks at anytime, even if the stock is plunging. A more important rule: You can't short a stock whose price is less than $5 a share.

Although selling short sounds like an easy strategy, a lot of things can go wrong. First, when you go long a stock, the most you can lose is everything you invested. I know, that's pretty bad. On the other hand, when you short a stock, you can lose more than you invested, which is why shorting can be risky. Let's see how this works.

If you sell short 100 shares of Bright Light at $20 a share, you receive $2000. If Bright Light drops to $18 a share, you made 2 points, or a $200 profit. Let's say you are wrong and Bright Light goes higher. For every point Bright Light goes up, you lose $100. How high can Bright Light rise? The answer is frightening: infinitely! The problem with shorting is that if the stock goes up, not down, your losses are incalculable.

I knew a group of guys who shorted Yahoo! in 1997 when it reached $90 a share. They were convinced that Yahoo! was overpriced. Perhaps they were technically correct, but that didn't stop the stock from soaring to as high as $400 one year later. (It actually went over $1000 in 1999, or a *split-adjusted* price of $445.) These guys were forced to buy back the shares early, losing over 100 points, because the losses grew so large. A few years later, after the market came to its senses, Yahoo! dropped to less than $20 a share (adjusted for splits), but it was too late for my acquaintances.

Personally, I find it very enlightening to listen to short sellers. Too often, investors delude themselves into thinking that the market will always go higher. Professional short sellers are good at poking holes in the "too-good-to-be-true" proclamations of market bulls. In my opinion, you should listen to both sides of an argument, but in the end you should do what you think makes the most sense.

Other Ways to Classify Stocks

Outstanding Shares

As you remember, corporations issue shares of stock, which are made available to investors through a stock exchange. The total number of shares that a corporation has issued is called its *outstanding shares.* (I agree it's not the most exciting name.) In a real-life example, you might ask someone in the corporation, "What is the number of outstanding shares?"

To save yourself time, you could also look up the number of outstanding shares on the Internet—for example, at Yahoo! Finance. Keep in mind that the bigger the corporation, the more outstanding shares there are. Because the stock market goes up and down based on supply and demand, a corporation doesn't want to issue too many shares unless it is pretty sure that people will scoop them up.

Let's say that over a 10-year period, Microsoft issues a total of 1 billion shares to the public and to corporate insiders; therefore, the number of outstanding shares for Microsoft is 1 billion shares. (It is up to the board of directors of Microsoft to decide how many shares it wants to issue.) Obviously, the board keeps millions of shares of the stock for the company's officers and employees. Because they are company insiders, they got the shares at extremely low prices, perhaps for a few dollars a share. (This is one of the reasons that so many people who worked at Microsoft became millionaires.) In addition, the board of directors also sets aside millions of shares to be used for equipment, computers, and research and development.

The Float

The total number of shares issued by the corporation is called the outstanding shares. Can you guess what the shares are called when we refer only to those owned by outside investors like you and me? Those shares are called the *float*.

I'll explain this as simply as possible. Let's say a corporation has a total of 5 million outstanding shares. Of those 5 million shares, corporate insiders hold 3 million. The question of the day: How many shares have been allocated to outside investors to be actively traded? If you guessed 2 million shares, you're right. The float is 2 million shares. These are the shares that are traded every day on the stock exchange by investors and traders.

Why Outstanding Shares and Float Are Important

Although some people don't care how many shares are outstanding or what the float is, others think this information is extremely important. Why? Keep in mind that the market is all about supply and demand. If you know how many shares are outstanding and what the float is, you can calculate whether there is too little supply and too much demand (the stock will go up in price) or too much supply and not enough demand (the stock price will go down). Also, it's a good idea for new investors to become familiar with market vocabulary.

Market Capitalization

Another way to classify stocks is by size. The *market capitalization* (*market cap*) of a stock tells you how large the corporation is. (To calculate market cap, you multiply the number of outstanding shares by the current stock price. Therefore, the market cap of a stock varies depending on both the number of outstanding shares and the stock price. For example, a large corporation with 10 billion outstanding shares and a stock price of $50 has a market cap of $500 billion.)

Some people will invest only in large-cap stocks (those of large corporations worth more than $5 billion), which include the stocks of corporations like Coca-Cola, Alcoa, and Johnson & Johnson, because they feel that the stocks of these corporations are safer and the corporations will never go bankrupt. (This isn't always true, however, since the fifth largest company in the country, Enron Corporation, filed for bankruptcy in 2002.) Other investors are attracted to mid-cap stocks (those of medium-sized corporations worth between $1 and $5 billion), while still others invest in small-cap or microcap stocks (those of small corporations worth between $250 million and $1 billion) because they cost less and their price often moves quickly.

When you compare the stock price to the market cap, you can see how difficult it is for large-cap stocks to double or triple. For example, let's say you own shares in a $50 large-cap stock of a company with a market cap of $500 billion. In order for the stock price to double, the company would have to increase in value from $500 billion to $1 trillion—not impossible, but extremely difficult and time-consuming. One reason some investors prefer small-cap stocks is that there is a better chance that they will double or triple. On the other hand, the smaller the stock's market cap, the higher the risk.

The IPO

Stocks that are being sold to the public for the first time are called *initial public offerings,* or *IPOs.* (Wall Street refers to this process as "going public.") The IPO is an exciting time for the corporation. The biggest advantage of going public for a company is that it allows the company to raise money. It can use this money to expand, to pay off debt, or to pay for research and development of a new product. In addition, if the IPO is successful, it can make company insiders extremely rich. There are two types of IPOs, the start-up (a company that never existed before) and the private company that decides to go public.

The corporation will appoint a major Wall Street stock brokerage firm (identified as the lead underwriter) to manage the IPO process and bring the stock to market. Investment bankers who work for the brokerage firm will determine how many shares of stock to issue to the public and what price to set.

Before the company goes public, early investors are given a chance to buy the stock at cut-rate prices. For example, corporate insiders could get thousands of shares of the stock for a dollar. Meanwhile, investment bankers will work with the underwriters to try to create investor interest in the corporation. Once the company goes public, research analysts that work for the underwriter may issue buy recommendations on the stock and make positive comments about the corporation.

We all saw the power of the Internet stocks when Netscape went public in April 1995. The lead underwriter, a major New York brokerage firm, calculated that the stock would be worth $28 a share. Minutes after the stock opened for the day, it rose to $75 a share, a price move that surprised many on Wall Street (although in later years some Internet IPOs rose by even more— for example, in 1998 TheGlobe.com went from $9 to $87 in one day, and in 1999, an IPO called VA Linux jumped 700 percent in one day, opening at $30 and rising to a high of $299). For the next 5 years, any stock that had anything to do with the Internet was given a robust reception by Wall Street. The demand for these Internet stocks was nothing short of phenomenal.

Like all good things, however, the fun ended after a few years. Most of the Internet stocks made a round trip back to their original price, and many went out of business. For example, a few years after its IPO, VA Linux was trading for less than $5, and TheGlobe.com was recently at less than a dollar. In addition, many of those who bought Internet IPOs on the first day lost thousands of dollars because they bought too high.

As an individual investor without inside connections, it is probably best if you avoid buying IPOs. More than likely, you will end up buying at the top and be forced to sell at a loss. Although some traders made small fortunes on IPOs on the way up, the IPO game is difficult to win, unless you are a company insider and buy early shares.

If you do want to participate in an IPO, however, be sure you read the *prospectus,* a legally binding document filed with the

SEC, that includes the company's future plans as well as its current financial condition. To cover themselves, startup companies will mention, often in small print, that there are no guarantees the company will succeed and there are tremendous risks. After reading all the risks, you may decide not to invest in the company at all!

In the next chapter, you will learn everything you need to know about stock prices.

Understanding Stock Prices

Many people think that all they have to know about a stock is its share price. While this is an important piece of information, it's only one piece of the puzzle. Nevertheless, stock price is important. After all, since the stock market is an auction, you should know how much a stock costs, and most important, what it's worth before you buy or sell it.

Basic Stock Quote

A stock quote (or quotation) is simply the current price of a stock. An example of a stock quote is given in Figure 5-1.

If you don't know the current price of a stock, you can simply ask your broker, for example, "Could you give me a quote for Cisco?" In the example in Figure 5-1, the person will reply, "$15.04." This simply means that if you wanted to buy one share of Cisco at that moment, it would cost you $15.04. For many people, the stock quote is the most important piece of information they can receive about a stock; it tells them exactly how much it will cost them to buy the stock, or what they will receive if they sell it.

Symbol	Last Trade		Change		Volume
CSCO	9:49am	**15.04**	+0.21	+1.42%	6,007,203

Chart, Financials, Historical Prices, Industry, Insider, Messages, News Options, Profile, Reports, Research, SEC Filings, ***more*** *...*

Figure 5-1

For years, some stock exchanges were unwilling to give out real-time stock quotes and news unless they were paid exorbitant fees for the information. Individual investors who didn't pay the fees received free stock quotes, but with a 20-minute delay.

Today, however, it's very easy to get free real-time stock quotes any time of the day or night. You can look on financial television programs like CNBC, Bloomberg, or CNNfn. If that is inconvenient, you can pick up the phone and call your stockbroker (if you have one). If you are patient, you can always wait for tomorrow's newspaper. The easiest way of checking stock quotes is by logging on to the Internet. There are hundreds of financial sites that provide real-time quotes.

As you can see in Figure 5-1, each stock has it own ticker symbol. (In addition to stocks, mutual funds, index funds, bonds, and options have ticker symbols.) Some are easy; for example, the stock symbol for IBM is IBM. The symbol for Microsoft is MSFT, that for AT&T is T, that for General Electric is GE, and that for Cisco Systems is CSCO. If you aren't sure of the exact ticker symbol, type in the name of the company, and the computer will give you the ticker symbol in seconds.

Most people refer to a stock by its symbol rather than its full name. Every experienced investor has memorized the ticker symbols for the most popular stocks. You can tell what exchange the stock is listed on by counting the number of letters in the symbol. If the stock is on the Nasdaq, the symbol will have 4 or 5 letters. If the stock is on the NYSE, it will have 1, 2, or 3 letters.

Detailed Stock Quote

Let's take a look at a detailed stock quote for Cisco Systems (CSCO), shown in Figure 5-2.

Views: Basic - DayWatch - Performance - Real-time Mkt - Detailed - [Create New View]

CISCO SYSTEMS (NasdaqNM:CSCO) - Trade: Choose Brokerage

Last Trade	Change	Prev Cls	Open	Volume
9:49am–15.06	+0.23 (+1.55%)	14.83	15.12	6,103,711

Day's Range	Bid	Ask	P/E	Mkt Cap	Avg Vol
14.96–15.19	15.05	15.07	40.08	108.8B	81,647,045

52-wk Range	Bid Size	Ask Size	P/S	Div/Shr	Div Date
8.12–21.92	22,300	10,400	5.55	0.00	22-Mar-00

1y Target Est	EPS (ttm)	EPS Est	PEG	Yield	Ex-Div
15.34	0.37	0.54	1.27	N/A	23-Mar-00

Chart, Financials, Historical Prices, Industry, Insider, Messages, News Options, Profile, Reports, Research, SEC Filings, more . . .

Figure 5-2

Bid: This is the price you will receive if you want to sell the stock.
Ask: This is the price you will pay if you want to buy the stock.
Previous Close: The stock closed at this price on the previous day.

When you look at the detailed stock quote in Figure 5-2, you will see two stock prices, one higher than the other. These are the *bid price* and the *ask price*. The bid and ask prices are extremely important but also confusing (at least they were to me).

The lower price (the one on the left) is the bid price (or offer price), which is the price you will receive if you own the stock and want to sell it. In Figure 5-2, the bid price for Cisco is $15.05. The higher price (on the right) is the ask price, the price you will have to pay if you want to buy this stock. The ask price for Cisco is $15.07.

The difference between the bid and ask prices is called the *spread*. In Figure 5-2, the difference between the bid price ($15.05) and the ask price ($15.07) is 0.02. A few years ago, when stock quotes were in fractions, the spread on some stocks was very high, sometimes as much as a dollar.

When the spreads were very wide, if you bought a stock and then sold it quickly, you would immediately lose money on the spread. The lower the spread, the better for investors. Because of *decimalization* (instead of displaying stock quotes in fractions, the exchanges now display them in decimals), the spread between the bid and ask prices is often quite small, sometimes only a penny or two. That makes it fairer for investors.

Other important information is how much the stock has risen or fallen in both absolute and percentage terms during the day. In Figure 5-2, Cisco is up 0.23, or 1.55 percent. Many people also look at the 52-week lows and highs to get an idea of where the stock price has been in the past.

The detailed stock quote also gives the market capitalization, the outstanding shares, how much dividend the company pays (if any), and the volume. (In the detailed stock quote example, note that you can do a historical price search as well as do extensive research on any stock or mutual fund.) You can learn a lot by studying the detailed stock quote.

Stock Price

Keep in mind that the detailed stock quote is just a quick snapshot of what is happening with the stock. Although these numbers can be useful, if you want to really get to know a stock, you'll have to dig deeper, as you'll learn as you read the rest of the book. A lot of people don't realize that the stock price is just one small piece of information you need to know about a stock. Some claim that it's the least important piece!

Too many people believe that the stock price determines whether a stock is a bargain or not. What many people don't realize is that a stock selling for $50 can be a better value than a stock selling for $10. If the $10 stock has little or no earnings and loads of debt, you'd be better off buying fewer shares of the $50 stock rather than more shares of the $10 stock. (Warren Buffett once said, "It's far better to buy a wonderful company at a fair price than a fair company at a wonderful price.") That's why some investors spend so much time looking at ratios like the P/E (when you divide a stock price by its earnings per share, you end up with a P/E, or price/earnings, ratio) to determine what is a fair price.

After all, you don't want to be the kind of person who knows the price of everything but the value of nothing (to paraphrase Oscar Wilde).

After-Hours Trading: Making Money 24 Hours a Day

During the bull market, a lot of people, myself included, thought that people would flock to the after-hours market. We figured that people who couldn't trade during the day would be eager to trade at night. As the markets fell, so did interest in after-hours trading. In the middle of the bull market, online and traditional brokerage houses were aggressively offering clients the ability to trade at any time of the day or night. But as the market plummeted and investors lost money, the after-hours market fizzled out. Although professional traders continue to trade at night, only a handful of investors still participate in the after-hours market. (The after-hours market also includes the *premarket,* which usually begins around 8:00 a.m. EST.)

After-hours trading works like this: The major stock exchanges remain open for electronic trading through electronic communication networks (ECNs) so that investors can trade outside of regular hours.

Only a few million shares are traded in the after-hours market, unlike the regular market, where billions of shares are traded during the day. In fact, the volume is so small that most investors would be well advised to avoid night trading altogether (unless you take the time to thoroughly understand how it works). The low volume can cause strange things to happen to stock prices. If you are unfamiliar with after-hours trading, you can end up buying or selling a stock for a terrible price. Trading after hours is a tricky strategy, and my advice is to do most of your investing and trading during the regular market.

In the next chapter, you will learn how to buy and sell stock.

Where to Buy Stocks

Although buying and selling stocks is easy, making money at it is hard work. Many very smart people have tried and failed to beat the market. If you've never invested in the market before, there is no need to rush. The stock market will be there when you're ready. The first step is to open an account with a brokerage firm.

You may wonder how much money you need in order to get started. (Some will say that you should invest only what you can cheerfully afford to lose.) You can start investing in the market with $5000 or less, although it will be harder for you to diversify and thus reduce your risk. With $5000 or more, it's possible to create a fairly well diversified portfolio.

Full-Service Brokerage Firm: Bells and Whistles for a Price

Full-service brokerage firms include some of the largest and most influential stock brokerage firms on Wall Street. These firms provide a huge variety of financial and investment products. They pretty much have it all, offering you investment advice, research, banking services, and the ability to buy and sell stocks, bonds, mutual funds, and fixed-income products like CDs. Although the full-service firms are particularly interested in attracting a wealthy clientele, anyone can open an account. Just don't expect to receive a high level of personalized service unless you have a large portfolio.

If you open an account with a full-service brokerage firm, you will be assigned a person to handle your account. (Some of these companies also have an online brokerage division that caters to do-it-yourself investors.) Such people used to be called stockbrokers, but because unscrupulous brokers gave the industry a bad reputation, they now refer to themselves in a variety of creative ways: financial advisers, financial consultants, account executives, or money managers.

Stockbrokers not only are paid to advise you what stocks to buy or sell but will personally fill the order. For this service, they are paid a commission on each trade; the commission on one trade can easily cost you several hundred dollars. You are basically paying the broker to oversee your portfolio and provide investment advice. Stockbrokers at full-service firms often have access to research reports that are supposed to be more detailed and accurate than the information that is released to the public.

The problem with the commission-based system is that it is in the best interest of brokers to see to it that you buy or sell frequently because the more you trade, the larger the commissions that they receive. (Some stockbrokers have been known to urge clients to buy or sell a lot so that they could get more commissions. This well-known but illegal practice is called *churning*.) It is also in the broker's best interest to direct you toward products that provide the highest commissions.

If you do hire a stockbroker, my advice is to find an honest, competent individual who truly cares about your investment portfolio. What you don't need is fast-talking salesperson who wants to make money for the firm by generating bigger commissions. Many retail stockbrokers, in my opinion, don't have the time or knowledge to give you top-notch investment advice. On the other hand, a skilled stockbroker can definitely do wonders for your portfolio.

In response to complaints about the commission-based system, some brokerages have changed their fee structure for clients with large portfolios. Instead of charging commissions on each trade, they now charge a 1 or 2 percent annual fee. In the end, it is really your choice whether a full-service stock brokerage meets your needs. It is a decision you should take seriously, since it's your money at stake.

The 1987 Stock Market Crash: Electronic Trading Is Born

Before 1987, the only way you could trade stocks was by calling your stockbroker on the phone (unless you were one of the lucky few who had enough money to buy a seat on one of the stock exchanges). The weakness of this system was revealed in October 1987, when the U.S. markets crashed, falling by more than 20 percent in one day.

Because many investors and institutional investors panicked and tried to sell at the same time, the phone lines jammed or stockbrokers refused to answer their phones. On more than a few occasions, the floor brokers filled the orders of institutional investors but ignored orders from individual investors. (As you can imagine, many investors lost everything because they sold too late.)

Because of this fiasco, the Nasdaq created a special computerized system called SOES (Small Order Execution System) that allowed traders to place orders electronically and at the most competitive price. The first to take advantage of SOES were day traders, who discovered that they could bypass a stockbroker and send their orders directly to the stock exchange. This was the beginning of the online trading revolution, but it was only for day traders. It was another 10 years before retail investors were allowed to trade online.

Online Investing and Trading: Saving Money on Commissions

Before people traded stocks on the Internet, they could save money by going to discount brokerages. Discount brokerages were geared toward the do-it-yourself investor who wanted low commissions. In return for low commissions, these brokers provided minimal advice and little research.

The Internet, however, changed Wall Street forever. Discount brokers were the first to connect their customers to the Internet. For extremely low commissions, people could trade stocks from the comfort of their own homes via the Internet without first contacting a stockbroker. Although there are still discount and deep discount brokers, as far as many people are concerned, they are all online brokerages.

Online investing or *online trading* simply means that you buy and sell online from your own computer. When you open an account with an online firm, you will not receive investment advice. That's the price you pay for commissions that are sometimes less than $10 a trade. Because of increased competition, online brokers will give you instant quotes, stock charts, and interactive research. You can open an online account with an online trading brokerage for as little as a few hundred dollars.

The downside to opening an account with an online brokerage is that some people desperately need investment advice. (Many people thought it was easy to make money online, and it was—until the recent bull market ended.) If you're looking for advice, or you have a huge portfolio, an online broker might not be right for you.

What Happens after You Open a Brokerage Account?

The retail brokerage firm or online brokerage sends you an enrollment packet with forms to fill out. After you send the firm a check or money order, it usually puts your money into a money market account, which is similar to a savings account. It usually takes about 10 days for your account to become active.

The Types of Orders You Can Place with a Brokerage Firm

Before you buy your first stock, you need to know what kind of order to place. It is essential that you learn the vocabulary so that you'll be able to communicate with your stock brokerage.

Market Order: Fast Fills but Not the Best Price

The fastest and easiest type of order is a *market order*. It is also the most common. Let's say we look up the stock quote on Bright Light (BRLT) and see that it is trading at $20 by $20.25. To refresh your memory, if you wanted to buy Bright Light, the current market price is $20.25, which is how much you would have to pay if you wanted to buy it right now. You don't like that price? Don't worry—it will change in a second. (It's kind of like Chicago weather.)

When you pay the market price for a stock, it is filled fast. Why? Because the people selling it to you know that the price they're giving you is the best price for them. It's kind of like buying a car and paying the list price. If you want the stock quickly, you pay the market price. Just remember that you are paying a little bit more for the speed.

Let's take a closer look at the other kinds of orders you can place.

Limit Order: Slower Fills at Competitive Prices

There is another type of order that is a little more complicated but that allows you to negotiate a better price—the *limit order*. The advantage of a limit order is that you can decide for yourself the price at which you want to buy or sell the stock. The disadvantage is that a limit order often takes more time to fill. In fact, it may never be filled, especially if the price you picked is too low or too high.

Here's how the limit order works: Let's say Bright Light is trading at $20 a share and you want to buy it, but you feel you could get it for a better price. Instead of buying it at the market price, $20, you put an order in to buy it at a limit price of $19. If Bright Light ever falls to $19, then the order will be initiated and filled at the current market price. If the stock never makes it to $19, then your order won't be filled.

You have a couple of choices when you enter a limit order. For example, let's say you place a limit order to buy 100 shares of Bright Light at $19 a share (even though it's selling for $20 a share). At this time, you must specify whether the order is good for the day only (day order) or good until you cancel the order (good-till-canceled order, or GTC). If you select good-till-canceled, you can go about your business and not worry about the order until it's filled one day in the future. With a day order, if the brokerage can't fill your order that day, it will be automatically canceled at the end of the day.

Sometimes, for whatever reason, no matter where you put your limit order, you never seem to get it filled at the most competitive price. Nevertheless, the limit order gives you a lot more flexibility. If you really want to shop around, you can put in limit orders for almost any price you want. For example, you could put in a low-ball offer at 10 points below the current stock price. (If your order does get filled, however, there's nothing to stop the stock from going even lower.)

Stop-Loss Order: Protecting You from Financial Disaster

As the name implies, the purpose of a *stop-loss order* is to protect your profits (if the stock is a winner) or to cut your losses (if the stock is a loser). A stop-loss order instructs your brokerage to sell the stock at a price that you specify. In real life, it works like this: Let's say you buy Bright Light at $20 a share. At the time you buy the stock, you place a stop-loss order at $18 a share. This means that if Bright Light drops to $18 a share, the brokerage will automatically sell your shares, and your loss is limited to approximately 10 percent. (The order is guaranteed to be executed, but there is no guarantee that it will be at the exact price you want.)

Many people don't believe in stop-loss orders. They think that if a stock falls in price, this is a good opportunity to buy, not to sell. One well-known fund manager said that stop-loss orders can chip away at your portfolio—like death by a thousand cuts.

The stop-loss order isn't perfect, of course. In volatile markets, for example, your stop-loss order can be filled inadvertently. Here's what can happen: You set up a stop loss at $18 a share (using Bright Light as an example). A couple of hours later, Bright Light drops to $18, and the stop loss is triggered. At first, you're relieved because you sold before the stock fell any further. Unfortunately, after being down as much as 10 percent, Bright Light rallies to $22 a share, but you have already sold for a loss.

Some people solve this problem by using a "mental" stop loss (some people write it on paper). Unfortunately, most investors do not have the discipline to sell a stock when it hits the target price. They freeze in fear when their beloved stocks fall by dozens of points, or they convince themselves that the lower price is only temporary. Others won't get rid of their losing stocks because "they are too cheap to sell."

The bottom line: Before you buy a stock, think in advance about when you'll sell it in case you are wrong. A stop-loss order is like an insurance policy that you use when the unexpected happens. It can help to prevent you from losing everything. (At some brokerages, you can place a trailing stop order that rises as the stock price goes up.)

You can also place a *stop limit order,* which is similar to a stop-loss order except that after the specified price is hit, the order becomes a limit order instead of a market order. With a stop limit order, you enter two prices: the stop price and the limit price. I know this sounds confusing, but it becomes clear after a few weeks of practice.

Placing Your First Order

Ready to have some fun? Let's say you have filled out the necessary paperwork and opened an account with an online broker. Your beginning balance is $2500, which is sitting safely in a money market account. You are now at your computer, and you want to buy 100 shares of Bright Light at the market price. Fortunately, online brokers have made it very easy to buy and sell stocks. If you have a stockbroker, you call the stockbroker on the phone (most brokerages also allow you to enter the order on their Web site) to place your order.

If you have an online broker, you follow the on-screen instructions. Begin by typing the symbol for Bright Light (BRLT), type 100 shares, and select *market order.* (Be sure you don't make any mistakes.) After you press the Enter key, the computer does the rest. A lot of what then happens to your order depends on the stock you pick.

A minute ago, Bright Light was trading at $20.25. Now it's at $21.00. Because you placed a market order, it is immediately filled. The brokerage firm automatically transfers $2100 from your money market account to buy 100 shares of Bright Light for $21.00 a share. The brokerage also deducts a commission of $9.99. Congratulations! You are now a Bright Light shareholder. If Bright Light goes up a point, you have what we call a paper gain of $100. Not a bad way to make a living, is it? Now you can go to the beach or to work and watch your money make money. Instead of your working for your money, your money is working for you.

Order Routing: How Your Order Is Sent

As mentioned earlier, if you chose to buy a NYSE stock, the order is routed to a *specialist* on the exchange, who fills your order electronically. If you buy a Nasdaq stock, a market maker will also handle the order electronically. More than likely, no matter which stock you choose, your order will be routed to an ECN (electronic communication network), where it will be matched electronically.

As an investor (not a day trader), you care only that your order is executed quickly and for a reasonable price. Some online brokers who cater to day traders offer "price improvement," which means that their software will find the most competitive price. There is also special trading software that allows you to specify who will handle your orders. This software, called *Level II*, allows you to see the names of all market makers, specialists, and ECNs. Then you can pick the most competitive price.

Unless you are an experienced trader or the software is provided for free, there's little reason to install Level II software. In most cases, your online broker will route your order to an ECN, where it will be handled as efficiently as possible. The best time to evaluate how quickly your broker handles your orders is during a fast-moving market. The best brokers are efficient under all market conditions.

Note: The best time to place an order is after 10:00 a.m. Eastern time. The reason is that professional traders and institutional investors often use their own money to force prices in the direction they want them to go. Often, the market moves aggressively in one direction, only to reverse course an hour later. In general, if you are new to the stock market, avoid placing orders in the middle of the night or during the first half-hour and the last half-hour.

If You Don't Have the Money

When a brokerage firm lends you money to buy stocks, it's called "going on margin." *Margin* simply means that you are borrowing money from the brokerage firm so that you can buy additional shares of the same stock.

Usually, the brokerage will give you a 2-to-1 margin rate. For example, if you pay the brokerage $2000 to buy shares of Bright Light, the brokerage will lend you an additional $2000, allowing you to use a total of $4000 to buy shares of Bright Light. You will be charged interest on the extra $2000 that you borrowed at current interest rates.

The advantage of margin is that you are using other people's money (called *leveraging*) to make more money. This works great if your stock goes up in price. On the other hand, if your stock loses money, not only do you lose some or all of your original investment (which is painful enough), but you'll still owe all the money that you borrowed. In the stock market, stocks go down faster than they go up, so margin can be extremely dangerous.

In the 1920s, margin requirements were as low as 10-to-1, so if you had only $1000 to invest, the brokerage would lend you an additional $9,000. One of the reasons the market crashed in 1929 was because of margin. As the stock market fell, people who had bought stocks on margin didn't have the money to pay back what they had borrowed. That's when banks and brokerages stepped in to take possession of people's savings accounts, houses, and anything else they could get their hands on.

In 1934, President Franklin Delano Roosevelt created the Securities and Exchange Commission (SEC), the government agency charged with making sure that the stock market is run fairly and protecting investors. One of the rules the SEC agreed on was an increase in margin requirements.

If your stocks fall a lot while you are on margin, you might get the dreaded *margin call.* The brokerage will call you demanding that you provide more cash. If you don't move fast enough, the brokerage has the right to sell the stock until the margin percentage is at the proper levels (usually 30 percent or more). During the recent bear market, it is estimated that thousands of people were forced to liquidate their stocks because they couldn't come up with enough cash to support their margin accounts.

Most people don't have the discipline to handle margin correctly, which is why I think you should avoid it. In my opinion, margin is a dangerous tactic that is best left to professional traders. Invest what you can afford without borrowing from the brokerage to pump up your returns. If the only way you can invest in the market is with margin, you are gambling, not investing. You'll know what I mean after you receive your first margin call.

Electronic Communication Networks

Electronic Communication Networks (ECNs) are networks of computers that work behind the scenes to match buy and sell orders electronically. ECNs work in conjunction with the various stock exchanges to process your order faster, more efficiently (since there is no human interaction), and more cheaply. When ECNs were first introduced, they revolutionized the way stocks were traded and helped to lower commissions.

For a small fixed fee of pennies per share, the ECN acts as an electronic middleman. By going directly through an ECN, investors and traders avoid many of the financial games played by market makers and specialists. Although what happens to your order behind the scenes can be fascinating, most people are hardly aware that ECNs exist. As long as their order is filled quickly and cheaply, most investors don't care what happens to it.

The 1929 Stock Market Crash

"Those who cannot remember history are condemned to repeat it," warned philosopher George Santayana. There is no more glaring example than the 1929 stock market crash, which in some ways was eerily similar to the boom and bust cycle that the stock market went through beginning in March 2000.

It wasn't the Internet that fascinated the nation and helped usher in the roaring 1920s, it was electricity. At the same time, many people became enamored with the stock market. With very favorable margin rates (you could borrow 9 times the amount of your original investment), it seemed as if everyone was in the stock market. As more and more people entered the market, the prices of stocks went up. (In a way, it was like a huge Ponzi scheme. People paid off what they owed on their original investment with the paper profits they made on their rising stocks.)

The attitude of the Coolidge administration was laissez-faire, a French term meaning "letting things be." The government wanted to let the forces of capitalism work without interference. As the stock market got shakier and the economy got worse, the new president, Herbert Hoover, realized that something had to be done. The goal was to increase margin requirements (which many considered the main culprit) without causing panic. Unfortunately, the market panicked.

After a series of frightening stops and starts, the market finally crashed on October 24, 1929. Over $10 billion of investors' money was wiped out before noon. Huge crowds of angry and shocked investors packed the visitor's gallery of the NYSE to watch the debacle. By noon the market was in a "death spiral." Investors around the world were horrified at the extent of the financial damage. By October 29, 1929, all the market's gains from the past year had been wiped out. Eventually, the market fell 89 percent from its 1929 high of 381.

After the crash, economists tried to figure out what had gone wrong. It was obvious that many people had missed the signs the market was overpriced. For example, the P/Es of many stocks were high, well beyond what was considered the P/E safe zone of 15. In addition, the Fed decided to raise interest rates, which many economists considered to be the wrong move. Congress also had a hand in turning what really was a recession into a full-blown depression. For example, during this period it doubled income taxes and raised tariffs on imports and exports.

Another problem was that banks were allowed to operate with few restrictions on how much they could lend. After the crash, many of the banks' customers had no way of paying back the money they had borrowed, forcing many banks to close. Finally, many people believed that fraud and insider activity was to blame. After the initial crash, the United States entered a 3-year bear market; the Dow finally bottomed at 41 in 1932.

The new president, Franklin Delano Roosevelt (FDR), took a number of unprecedented steps to bring stability and trust to the market, including creating the SEC in 1932. Wall Street was skeptical about letting the government interfere with the private sector, but the steps the goverment took eventually helped turn the economy around. However, it took 25 years for the Dow to make it back to 381.

In the next chapter, you will learn how to build wealth over time by using long-term investment strategies.

PART TWO

MONEY-MAKING STRATEGIES

7

Want to Make Money Slowly? Try These Investment Strategies

As mentioned in the first chapter, a strategy is a plan that helps you determine what stocks to buy or sell. If you are new to the stock market, it's best to keep an open mind before choosing a strategy. If a particular strategy seems to make sense to you, take the time to do more research. It can take a long time before you find an investment strategy that not only makes sense but also increases the value of your portfolio. Keep in mind that you aren't limited to only one strategy. Some investors and traders use a variety of strategies, whereas others are comfortable using only one. No matter what strategy you use, here are a few things you should remember:

1. A strategy is only as good as the person using it. In other words, no matter how brilliant and ingenious the strategy, you can still lose money.
2. Not all strategies work during all market conditions.

3. Don't become so devoted to a strategy that you are blind to the fact that you are losing money. Money is the scorecard that determines whether your strategy is working.

You have to take the time to find the strategy or strategies that fit your personality and lifestyle. Unfortunately, there are no magic answers to finding success in the stock market. For most people, the only way to find out what ultimately works on Wall Street is through trial and error.

Buy and Hold: The Most Popular Strategy for Investors

The reasoning behind the buy-and-hold strategy is that if you buy a stock in a fundamentally sound company and hold it for the long term (at least a year), you'll realize a profit. The beauty of a buy-and-hold strategy is that you can buy a stock and watch it rise in price without having to constantly watch the market. Investors who bought companies like IBM, GE, and Microsoft in the early days made huge sums of money on paper without having to pay much attention to the market. The other advantage of buy and hold is that because you are not constantly buying and selling stocks, you are paying very little in brokers' commissions. Buy and hold is the easiest investment strategy to use, and, in retrospect, it worked extremely well during the bull market of the 1990s.

Perhaps the only time buy-and-hold investors sell is if something fundamentally changes in a company. They don't sell because of what is happening to the market, the economy, or the stock price. They are focused only on the business, and they intend to hold their reasonably priced stocks as long as possible.

One of the most successful buy-and-hold investors of the twentieth century is billionaire Warren Buffett. He rarely buys stocks in technology companies, but rather buys the stocks of mundane companies such as insurance companies and banks, and he has the skill (along with a team of independent analysts) to buy low and sell high.

In the hands of a professional, buy and hold can work, although many investors who used this strategy ended up losing their shirts during the recent bear market. Rather than buying low-priced value stocks, they bought and held high-priced technology stocks. Buy and hold does work, but it's not as easy to use as people think.

Buy on the Dip: An Offshoot of Buy and Hold

The buy-on-the-dip strategy was also very popular during the 1990s. In this strategy, when a stock you like goes down in price, especially if you believe the decline is only temporary, you buy more shares. The idea is that because the market always goes up over time (or generally has in the past), the shares you bought at a lower price will eventually be worth more. People who used this strategy in the past made tons of money as the shares they bought kept going higher.

The problem with buying on the dip is that stocks sometimes dip two or three times before dropping permanently. In the late 1990s, millions of people poured their life savings into stocks that seemed like bargains but actually were extremely overpriced. With every dip, more buyers stepped in. Then, during the 2000 bear market, many of these stocks didn't just make a temporary dip, they crashed. During the bear market, the stocks that made up the Nasdaq fell by over 80 percent. It is still too early to know if these stocks will ever return to the price levels they were at before.

Bottom Fishing: Finding Bargains among Unloved Stocks

If you are a bottom fisher, you look for stocks that are so low that they seem to have hit bottom. Professional bottom fishers are constantly on the lookout for stocks that are so low that they have nowhere to go but up.

The danger of bottom fishing is that you never know exactly when the bottom has been reached. For example, when Enron went from nearly $100 a share to $15, many people bought more shares, assuming that the stock couldn't go much lower. When the stock was trading at $1 a share, the bottom fishers stepped in. The stock then fell almost 94 percent before really hitting bottom, finally closing at 6 cents. You also face the danger that companies like Enron will eventually go out of business.

Because it could be years before many of these unloved stocks rise in price, you have to be extremely patient to be a successful bottom fisher. Stocks that are in the basement tend to stay there a while. (Many bottom fishers will wait 2 or 3 years before scooping up favorite stocks that other investors have ignored.)

Dollar-Cost Averaging: A Systematic Stock-Buying Approach

Instead of buying stocks whenever you have extra money in your pocket, with *dollar-cost averaging* you buy stocks on a regular, systematic basis. You invest a set amount of money, perhaps $100, each set period of time—for example, each month. The beauty of this system is that as you buy stocks that are dropping in price, your average price per share also drops.

For example, let's say you buy 100 shares of Bright Light at $20. The next month it drops to $10, so you buy another 200 shares. Your average cost is now $13.33 a share. As long as the market keeps bouncing back, dollar-cost averaging is a winning strategy. The problem is that if your stocks keep dropping, you will be left with substantial losses.

A strategy similar to dollar-cost averaging is called *averaging down*. With this strategy, instead of investing a set amount of money each set period, you buy additional shares of stock on the way down. With dollar-cost averaging, you have a plan. With averaging down, you buy additional shares of stock whenever you please.

Value Investing: Buying Good-Quality Companies at a Cheap Price

Value investors primarily use fundamental analysis to pick good-quality stocks that are a bargain compared with their actual worth. In other words, value investors are looking for stocks that are on sale. Often, value investors will buy stocks in companies that other investors don't want. These are the low-P/E stocks of companies whose earnings grow slowly, such as insurance companies and banks. Value investors are long-term investors and are willing to wait years for their stocks to become profitable.

During the 1990s, value investors were ridiculed for not buying the high-flying technology stocks. While some growth stocks were doubling or tripling in price, many value stocks were producing what some considered pitiful returns. Ironically, after the 1990s ended, value stocks were back in favor. It seemed as though everyone wanted to buy fairly valued stocks in companies run by competent and honest managers that showed signs of improved earnings performance.

Growth Investing: Buying Growing Companies

In general, growth investors use fundamental analysis to find stocks that are growing faster than the economy or earning more than other stocks in the same industry. Growth investors like to see earnings growing by at least 15 or 20 percent a year for the next 3 or 4 years. Most important, these companies' earnings are growing faster than those of other companies in competitive industries. Usually, these stocks don't pay dividends because whatever extra money the company earns is plowed back into the company.

For many years, *growth investing* worked spectacularly well. Investing in growth stocks, particularly technology and Internet companies, was all the rage during the 1990s. It was not uncommon for investors to see returns of 100 percent or more per year. Although investing in growth stocks can be risky, the rewards can be tremendous.

An offshoot of growth investing is called *growth at a reasonable price* (GARP). Investors who engage in this strategy basically combine value and growth investing into one strategy. They are looking for growth stocks, but they are willing to wait until they can get the stocks at a reasonable price.

Momentum Investing: Buy High and Sell Higher

Momentum investors are growth investors who look for stocks that are ready to make explosive moves upward. They buy stocks at a high price but plan to sell them at an even higher price. They don't care too much about the price they paid as long as the stock goes higher. Momentum investing works best during bull markets when there is a lot of liquidity. In the late 1990s, it seemed as if no matter which stock you bought—especially if was an Internet stock—the stock would go higher.

Some critics call momentum investing the "greater fool theory," which means that no matter how high the stock price is, you will always be able to find a bigger fool who is willing to buy it from you. Momentum investors tend to use technical analysis to look for stocks that will make sudden and dramatic moves in a short period.

In the go-go 1990s, a surprise announcement or positive rumor could send stocks up 20 or 30 points in one day. Although it is still possible to find momentum stocks, it's not as easy as it was a few years ago. (And it's unlikely that we'll see that kind of market environment again for many years to come.)

Momentum investing, although exciting and potentially profitable, is a difficult strategy. Many momentum stocks can explode in either direction, often costing you a lot of money. Although it's possible to catch some of these stocks on the upside, it is definitely not as easy as it looks. (Perhaps you should wait for the next bull market before using a momentum strategy.)

Contrarian Investing: Doing the Opposite of Everyone Else

Contrarians, as they call themselves, use fundamental analysis to find high-quality companies with low P/Es that other investors have abandoned. The more unloved the stock, the more contrarian investors like it. When everyone else was accumulating technology stocks in the late 1990s, contrarians were buying out-of-favor companies like Waste Management (WMI) and Red Hat (RHAT). After many technology stocks imploded, contrarians were scooping up shares of stock in unloved companies like Xerox (XRX).

Contrarians are especially fascinated by a company that the media and other investors hate. However, it takes a tremendous amount of skill and patience to find formerly high-flying stocks that will once again outperform the market. In addition, it takes courage to buy stocks that no one else wants.

There is also a group of contrarian traders called "investolators" who use technical analysis, especially charts and institutional ownership, to find stock picks. Just like contrarian investors, investolators look for unloved companies that have hit bottom. Ted Warren coined the term *investolator* in the 1930s, combining the words *investor* and *speculator.*

CANSLIM: A Disciplined Method of Picking Stocks

William O'Neil, founder and publisher of *Investor's Business Daily,* designed a rule-based investing system called CANSLIM. What is most helpful about CANSLIM is that it combines both technical and fundamental analysis, although it leans more toward the technical. Each letter of CANSLIM stands for a characteristic of a winning stock:

C: Current quarterly earnings per share
A: Annual earnings increase
N: New products, new management, new highs
S: Supply and demand
L: Leader or laggard
I: Institutional sponsorship
M: Market direction

Ideally, a winning stock should have all of these attributes, according to what O'Neil wrote in his best-selling book *How to Make Money in Stocks.*

C: Buy stocks with large increases in current earnings, preferably 25 percent or more. The higher the earnings per share, the better. Buy stocks in companies with accelerating earnings, especially when compared to previous quarters or years.

A: Concentrate on stocks that have increased earnings per share every year for the last 3 years. In addition, look for stocks with recent quarterly earnings improvement. Stocks with strong earnings improvement will have a higher probability of success.

N: Look for companies that have introduced new products or changed management. In addition, using technical analysis, look for stocks that have consolidated for a while before breaking out to reach new price highs.

S: The stock market is all about supply and demand. Find stocks that are rising in price on rising volume, a signal that institutional investors might be buying. Trading volume should be 50 percent above normal. In addition, look for companies that buy back their own stock and upper-level managers who privately own shares in their company.

L: Buy the strongest stocks in an industry group or sector. There is no reason to buy weak stocks (the laggards) even if the price is lower. In particular, buy the strongest stocks in a weak market (what technicians call *relative strength*). You want the leading stocks in the strongest industries with a relative price strength of 80 or more (a statistic found exclusively in *Investor's Business Daily*).

I: Buy stocks that are also owned by institutional investors such as pension funds, banks, and mutual funds. Stocks with strong institutional support are liquid, so it's easy to enter and exit.

M: Study price and volume indicators to understand the strength and weakness of the market. Use stock charts to identify market tops and bottoms. Use technical analysis not to make predictions but to understand what the stock is doing right now.

In the next chapter, you will learn how to make money quickly using short-term trading strategies.

Want to Make Money Fast? Try These Trading Strategies

Many of the following strategies are popular with aggressive short-term traders who want to make money quickly by taking advantage of volatile stock prices. These traders primarily use technical analysis to look for profitable trading opportunities, although some of them confirm their picks using fundamental analysis before buying or selling a stock.

Day Trading: Buying and Selling in Minutes

Unlike investors, who may wait years before selling, day traders buy and sell within seconds, minutes, or hours. *Day trading* is an extreme trading strategy that involves constantly moving into and out of stocks. Using technical analysis, professional day traders try to anticipate where a stock will go in the near future and trade accordingly. Usually, day traders sell all their stocks and move to cash by the end of each day.

Day traders can trade from their home or trade stocks at a day trading firm, which provides high-speed telephone lines and customized trading software. Although there have always been day traders, this strategy became particularly popular during the late 1990s. In fact, so many people were trading stocks from home that they were called *online traders*.

An online trader can use a number of short-term strategies besides day trading. For example, *swing trading* involves buying a stock early in the week and selling it a few days later. Another short-term trading strategy, called *position trading*, is to buy stock and hold it for a few months. Some traders follow the trend of the market, buying when the market is trending up and selling when the market is trending down.

Even with the best equipment and software, however, only a small percentage of people are actually able to make money consistently by day trading. First, it takes an incredible amount of discipline, trading capital, and knowledge to be a successful day trader. Most people don't have the patience to sit by a computer all day and watch stock positions. Although day traders can make money on occasion, it is an extremely difficult game to play unless you have the power of a bull market behind you. (It was no coincidence that just before the Nasdaq topped out at 5000, thousands of people quit their jobs to become day traders—a clear signal that things were going to end badly.)

Market Timing: A Controversial and Difficult Strategy

If you thought day trading was hard, imagine being a market timer. With *market timing,* you predict in advance where a stock or the market is headed. Then you make your move before the market does. For example, if you believe that the market will rise in the next week, you will shift your money out of cash or bonds and into stocks. The idea is to shift your money to the most profitable investment *before* it goes up (something that is easier said than done).

Market timing is a risky strategy that can cost you if you make the wrong bet. To be a successful market timer, you have to know not only when to get into the market, but also when to get out, which is why so few traders are successful market timers. Timing the market is difficult for most people. That hasn't stopped people from trying, however. (You could argue that even buy and hold is a form of market timing because you are trying to time your purchase so that you buy low and sell high.)

Short the Rallies: The Opposite of Buy and Hold

A very effective, but rather risky, trading strategy is to short the rallies. Instead of buying more stock when the market falls (buying on the dip), you do the opposite: When the market or your stock goes up a lot, you sell short (that is, you sell the stock, then buy it back at a lower price). Shorting the rallies is extremely risky, although it worked quite well for several years. After all, stocks go down faster than they go up.

Nevertheless, keep in mind that successfully shorting the rallies takes a tremendous amount of time, skill, and patience. If you are wrong and the stock keeps rising, it takes considerable discipline to buy back the shares (called *covering your position*) for a small loss.

Exchange-Traded Funds: A Clever Way to Spice Up Your Portfolio

Trading exchange-traded funds (ETFs) has recently become popular with traders and investors, including many professionals. An ETF is an investment product that is similar to a mutual fund, but that trades like a stock. You can buy and sell ETFs on any major stock exchange just as you would a stock. For as little as $500 you can buy an ETF that tracks a specific index or sector. The most common ETFs are index funds, such as the stocks that make up the Nasdaq 100 (QQQQ), the S&P 500 (SPY), and the Dow Jones Industrial Average (DIA). Because of the sudden popularity of these investments, new ETFs are being created all the time. Just like those of stocks, prices of ETFs change continuously during the day.

The advantage of trading ETFs is that they are cheap, liquid, and tax-friendly. Because they consist of a basket of individual stocks, ETFs provide instant diversification. After all, it would be too costly and time-consuming to buy so many individual stocks on your own. Because they are similar to stocks, you buy or sell ETFs through your brokerage firm or Internet broker. Ultimately, it's easy for both investors and traders to find an ETF that meets their investment needs.

The disadvantages of trading ETFs are similar to those of trading stocks. You pay a commission when you buy or sell. In addition, because ETFs are relatively new, they haven't much of a track record. Although it takes time to learn how to trade ETFs successfully, it's worth your time to learn how this popular investment product works.

Trading on News

Like day trading, trading stocks based on the news is a difficult method to play and win. It's impossible to know how the market will react to news about your stocks. There is a wise old saying: Buy on the rumor and sell on the news. Often a stock will rise or drop in price in anticipation of a news event, such as an earnings release or a Fed meeting. Once the news is released, however, the stock will go in the opposite direction, which explains why it is so difficult to buy or sell stocks based on what is in the news.

In reality, news is coming at you from dozens of different directions: newspapers, magazines, the Internet, television, and friends. The hard part is figuring out which information is valuable and which should be ignored. It's amazing how wrong people (both professionals and amateurs) have been about the market. Most of what people tell you about the market is useless. Nevertheless, keep in mind that stocks go up or down based on what people perceive to be the truth.

Some people deliberately try to influence the direction of stocks by spreading false information about companies. A few years ago, a stock could rise or fall based on nothing more than a well-placed rumor in an Internet chat room. So many people lost money by trading on tips and rumors that they stopped listening, at least temporarily. When the next bull market appears (and it is likely to be a long wait), the scam artists will crawl from beneath the rocks to lure unsuspecting investors into losing money on stocks.

Trading Options

Although options are rather difficult to understand, with a little practice, they begin to make more sense. That's why many professional traders include option strategies in their portfolios. In particular, traders will use options to *hedge* their position (taking the opposite side of a trade to reduce risk). For example, if a trader is long a stock, he or she might use options to short the same stock. While options can seem a bit overwhelming even for experienced investors, I'll do my best to explain them so that they make sense.

Think of an option as a contract that gives you the right, but not the obligation, to purchase or sell an item. It could be a house, a commodity like oil or corn, or a stock. One type of stock option, for example, gives you the right to purchase a particular stock at a given price by a certain date. The wonderful part about options is that you don't have to own the stock to trade them. Options are also called derivatives because their price comes from, or is derived from, the stock price.

The two most popular types of options are the *call* and the *put*. A *call option* gives you the right to buy a stock at a specified price. A *put option* allows you the right to sell a stock at a specified price. You have the right to buy or sell the underlying stock, but most people don't exercise this right. They simply buy and sell the option. For a fraction of the price, you can control hundreds or thousands of dollars worth of stock.

For example, let's say Bright Light is selling for $20 a share. You like Bright Light, and you think it will rise to $25 a share. So you decide to buy a call option with a strike price of $25. (You can choose any strike price. The further away the strike price is from the current price, the cheaper the option. For example, an option with a $20 strike price will be more expensive than one with a $25 strike price.) If Bright Light does hit $25 or higher, you will be "in the money." The higher the stock goes, the more money you will make.

There is a catch, however. When you buy an option, you also have to specify an expiration date, usually from 1 to 3 months from the date of purchase. This means that Bright Light must rise to or above the strike price *before* the expiration date or you will lose your entire investment.

You also have the right to sell before the expiration date. (Some options double or triple within days, so it's wise to lock in a profit.)

When you call your broker (or enter your order online), you might say, "I would like to buy five June contracts with a strike price of $25 a share." Each contract is worth 100 shares of stock. In this case, Bright Light has to rise to $25 a share or higher before the third Friday in June for you to make a profit (although you could sell it before the expiration date for a profit). How much will this cost you? The farther away the expiration date, the more it costs. For example, the June contracts might cost you $2 each. If you buy five option contracts, it will cost you $1000 (500 shares times $2 each). The July contracts might be $4 each, (although keep in mind that the price changes constantly during the day). There are contracts for every month of the year.

So you buy the June contracts for Bright Light at $2 each, for a cost of $1000. (If you bought 500 shares of Bright Light stock, it would cost you $10,000—$20 a share times 500 shares. When you buy the option, it costs you only $1000. So for $1000 you are controlling $10,000 worth of stock.) Let's say Bright Light rises to $25 within a week. You are now "at the money." As the price of Bright Light goes higher, the price of the option rises. You can also *exercise* your right to buy Bright Light stock for $25 a share.

The downside to options is that a lot of things have to go right for you to make money. First, if Bright Light doesn't rise to $25 a share by the third Friday in June, you lose the entire $1000. The option will expire worthless; as a matter of fact, according to studies, most options contracts expire unexercised by the expiration date. After commissions and taxes, most speculators don't make a dime trading options.

Instead of buying a call option, you could always buy a put option. In this case, you are anticipating that the price of the stock will go down, not up. During the recent long bear market, people who bought and sold put options cleaned up, assuming that they sold before the expiration date.

The options game is a tough one to win. To make money on options, you have to be right about both the timing and the price direction of the underlying stock. If you're wrong on either count, you will lose your entire investment. However, if you are still fascinated by options and want to learn more, there are dozens of option strategies.

Ask your brokerage firm for the brochure *Characteristics and Risks of Standardized Options,* which explains in detail how options work and the risks you take by trading them.

Writing Covered Calls: An Advanced Option Strategy to Generate Income

There is an intriguing but somewhat confusing option strategy that actually works well in a sideways market. It's called *writing covered calls* on a stock that you already own. This is considered one of the most conservative option strategies because it lowers the *cost basis* of the stock that you own.

Writing covered calls works like this: You sell a call option on a stock that you own to a call buyer, giving the buyer the right to take the stock out of your account at the agreed-upon price. For example, let's say you own 500 shares of Bright Light, which is currently selling for $20 a share. You write 5 calls (or 500 shares) for Bright Light with a strike price of $25 a share. When you sell the calls, you immediately receive money from the call buyer. (If the calls were selling for $1 each, then $500 would be placed into your account.)

Let's see what happens next. If Bright Light never makes it to $25 a share by the expiration date, then you keep the $500 and the option expires worthless for the call buyer. You then can write another 5 calls for another $500. On the other hand, if Bright Light does make it to $25 a share, you still keep the $500, but your Bright Light stock will automatically be sold at $25 a share.

The ideal market environment for a call writer is one in which stocks are going sideways. In a sideways market, the stock is unlikely to go very high, which is why writing calls can be a consistent money-maker. Even if Bright Light falls in price and you are forced to sell it at a loss, you get to keep the $500, which is called the *premium.* Many investors write calls no longer than a month in advance.

What is the disadvantage of writing covered calls? First, think about what would happen if Bright Light were to keep going higher, perhaps to $30 or $35? You have already sold it at $25, and so you won't participate in the price spike. Second, many option traders are so focused on the premium that they don't pay attention to the underlying stock. If you make 10 percent on the premium but lose 40 percent on

the stock, you have lost money. That is why if you are going to trade
options, it is essential that you first understand how to trade stocks.

ETF Workshop: Trading the QQQQs

One of the skills of a professional trader is to search for ways to
make money during any market environment. Although it was
easy for people to book profits during a raging bull market, the
current indecisive market has been a lot more challenging on a
day-to-day basis. That is why experienced traders are always
looking for new and aggressive strategies to let them survive and
win in today's market.

One surprisingly effective strategy for both investors and
traders is trading the Nasdaq 100 index on the American Stock
Exchange, known as "the Qs" from its symbol, QQQQ. This
index consists of the largest and most actively traded stocks on
the Nasdaq. Many professional traders and investors have discovered the Qs, making it one of the most liquid stocks on the
American Stock Exchange.

There are a number of advantages to trading the Qs. With
just one stock, you are basically trading the entire Nasdaq market, and with a lot more control than if you owned a mutual fund.
In addition, the high liquidity of the Q's means that your order
will be filled quickly. And finally, because there is no uptick rule
with the Qs, you can short stocks even as they are falling. (The
uptick rule means that on traditional stocks you aren't allowed to
short a stock until there is an "uptick," or a temporary spike in the
price.)

The disadvantage of trading the Qs is that they don't move as
far or as fast as many traditional stocks. This, however, could also
be perceived as an advantage, since for a little less potential
profit, you are also reducing your risk. Keep in mind that because
trading the Qs is similar to trading a stock, it's easy to lose money
if you are on the wrong side of the trade.

One of the reasons that many individual investors avoid
investing in the Qs is that the index fell from a high of $100 a

share when it was introduced in 1999 to as low as $20 three years later. Obviously, anyone who shorted the Qs made a small fortune. If you aren't comfortable trading the Qs, you can also try its relatives, the SPY (S&P 500) or the DIA (Dow 30).

If you are a new short-term trader, the Qs are a fantastic way of learning how to trade the NASDAQ long or short with a little less risk. On most days, the Qs trade within a well-defined trading range. If you are an investor who thinks the Qs hit bottom at $20, you could buy shares for a long-term investment. In any of these situations, be sure to use protective stop losses.

In the next chapter, you will learn how investors use fundamental analysis to buy and sell stocks.

PART THREE

FINDING STOCKS TO BUY AND SELL

It's Really Fundamental: Introduction to Fundamental Analysis

The two main methods that people use to pick stocks are fundamental analysis and technical analysis. *Fundamental analysis* is the study of the underlying data that affect a corporation. *Technical analysis,* on the other hand, is the study of a stock's price.

Some of you may find that fundamental analysis is all you need in order to be a successful investor. After all, understanding and applying fundamental stock analysis helped make billionaire investor Warren Buffett a very rich man. In addition, successful mutual fund managers, such as Peter Lynch, Robert Rodriguez, and William Miller, to name a few, have also used fundamental analysis to find stocks in high-quality companies at bargain prices. If you want to learn about the stock market, you must have at least a basic understanding of fundamental analysis. It is worth your time to study it.

Fundamental Analysis: An Overview

When you buy a stock on the basis of fundamental analysis, you are not simply buying a piece of paper; rather, you are buying a piece of a corporation. If you're going to buy a stock, you should find out as much as you can about the corporation. This is the essence of fundamental analysis: You study the corporation to decide whether it is a worthwhile investment.

This includes looking at a number of factors, including the company's assets and liabilities, its earnings, the managers who are running the company, the competition, the kind of business the company is in, and the amount of debt it has. (You can find many of these items in the balance sheet, a brief financial report of the corporation that will be discussed shortly.) By using fundamental analysis, you should be able to pick out stocks that offer you the best chance for profits. You want to buy a stock whose price is reasonable when compared with its earnings—what fundamental analysts call "fair value."

You should know that fundamental analysis is one of the most popular methods of determining whether a stock is a good bargain or is better left alone. If you have done your homework and closely studied all aspects of a corporation, you should be rewarded with a higher stock price.

Nevertheless, fundamental analysis is merely a tool to help you find and evaluate which stocks offer good value. Like anything related to the stock market, this method is more art than science. Just because you use fundamental analysis doesn't mean that you'll make a lot of money in the market. The more methods you learn, however, the better. This will also give you a chance to determine whether fundamental analysis is right for you.

The Concepts behind Fundamental Analysis

Learn Everything You Can about the Industry

The first thing an investor has to determine when engaging in fundamental analysis is what industry to look at. If we are in the middle of a recession, when jobs are scarce and people are struggling to stay out of debt, you might look at recession-proof industries like food, oil, and retail. Once the country is out of the doldrums and jobs are plentiful, you take a look at industries like technology that could take the market higher. Peter Lynch, a successful fund manager of the 1980s and 1990s, got many of his stock ideas by watching where his children shopped at the mall. If you go to the mall and The Gap, Starbucks, Hott Topic, or Victoria's Secret is filled with shoppers, this is a clue that these stores are making money. This doesn't mean that you should run out and buy stock in one of these companies—first you should use fundamental analysis to find out everything you can about the company. You should also take the time to read the annual report, call investor relations for an investment packet, and log on to the company Web site. You don't want to invest a lot of money in a stock without finding out everything you can about the company's business. Ideally, the business will be simple and understandable with good long-term prospects for the future.

Identify the Leading Company

Once you have identified the industry you want to invest in, you want to choose companies that are stronger and more profitable than their competition. Let's say you want to invest in the retail sector because you believe (after careful research) that people will flock to discount stores that can save them money. What stores come to mind? Wal-Mart? Home Depot? Walgreen's? Exactly. Choose the stores that have name brand recognition and that advertise heavily. These companies are called *industry leaders*. If people are buying the company's products, the company's earnings will go up, which should cause the stock price to rise. To find industry leaders, you want to look for companies that have superior sales and earnings with little or no debt.

The financial newspaper *Investor's Business Daily* rates the relative strength of stocks in leading industries, giving them a score between 1 and 99. A relative strength rating higher than 90 is considered excellent. You can also find information about industry leaders in the *Value Line Investment Survey,* which can be found at the public library. (The *Value Line Investment Survey* has loads of information about individual stocks condensed on one page. Nearly all of the fundamental information you need to know about a stock can be found in this periodical.)

Talk to the Managers

Many investors who use fundamental analysis believe in talking to the CEO and company managers to get a feel for how the corporation is being run. Ideally, when you speak to management, you can ask how the business is doing, where it will be spending its money, and who its competitors are; you can also get insights about the corporation. Questioning managers is something that many professional fund managers do. They want to invest in companies with experienced, innovative managers who have a vision for the future. They try to avoid companies that have too much debt, are losing business to competitors, and have other liabilities (like lawsuits) that can affect earnings.

As an individual investor, it is highly unlikely that you will be able to sit down with the CEO or upper management to share a drink and a game of golf and to try to find out exactly what is going on in the corporation. And even if you could, it is doubtful that the CEO would say anything negative about the corporation. That is why management interviews are somewhat controversial and why some professional investors would rather study the balance sheet than talk with managers.

Company Insiders: Watch Them Closely

According to the SEC, officers and directors of a corporation who have access to proprietary information and people who own more than 10 percent of the corporation's stock are considered *corporate insiders.* You can get clues to how a stock will do by looking at whether insiders are buying or selling the stock. To find what insiders are doing, log onto Yahoo! Finance (finance.yahoo.com), CBS Marketwatch (www.marketwatch.com), or Bloomberg (www.bloomberg.com). In addition, the SEC's Web site, www.sec.gov, manages the EDGAR (Electronic Data Gathering Analysis and Retrieval) database, which contains many fascinating financial documents about the actions of insiders.

Some investors have created strategies that involve copying insiders. After all, insiders are more knowledgeable about the future prospects of the company than others are. On the other hand, there are problems with tracking insider transactions. Sometimes insiders buy or sell for reasons that have nothing to do with what is happening at the company. In addition, because of the way insider transactions are reported, you may not find out what insiders are doing until it is too late. For example, while the CEOs of Enron and WorldCom dumped millions of shares of stock in their companies, their action wasn't made public until the stocks were trading for pennies a share (insider reports are sometimes delayed by up to 3 months).

The Balance Sheet: Uncovering the Truth about a Company's Finances

A *balance sheet* is a report of the financial condition of a business, including items that only an accountant could love. And yet, to really understand the company you have invested in, you should study its balance sheet.

Unfortunately, most people buy stocks without taking the time to read the balance sheet. Just remember this: You shouldn't waste thousands of dollars investing in a company unless you know a few facts about it, like how much the company earns, how much it spends, and how much it owes. When you have found out the truth about a company's earnings, expenses, and debt, you'll have a better idea of whether you should buy its stock.

The balance sheet is found at the back of a company's annual report. You can also find any company's balance sheet by registering free at www.businessweek.com. Type in the stock symbol and select SEC filings. You can also log on to Edgar Online, a subscription-based service that allows you access to all SEC filings, including the quarterly *10-Q* filing and the annual *10-K* filing.

Let's take a quick look at some of the items on a balance sheet (which by no means includes everything):

1. Assets (what the company owns, such as cash, property, equipment, real estate, and accounts receivable)
2. Liabilities (what the company owes, such as declared and unpaid dividends and accounts payable)
3. Shareholders' equity, or net worth (assets minus liabilities)

Let's take a look at Bright Light's consolidated balance sheet, shown in Figure 9-1.

Bright Light Balance Sheet
      (in thousands)

	December 31, 2002	December 31, 2001
ASSETS		
Current Assets		
Cash and cash equivalents	1,196	1,098
Accounts receivables	1,637	1,367
Inventories	528	530
Deferred income taxes	158	120
Property and equipment	978	877
Other assets	325	103
Total Current Assets:	4,822	4,095
LIABILITIES AND STOCKHOLDER'S EQUITY		
Current Liabilities		
Accounts Payable	879	525
Accrued Expenses	578	502
Income taxes payable	186	179
Current Portion of Long-Term Debt	98	75
Total current liabilities:	1,741	1,281
Stockholder's Equity		
Common stock	1,567	1,567
Retained earnings	1,514	1,247
Total stockholder's equity:	3,081	2,814
Total liabilities and stockholder's equity:	4,822	4,095

Figure 9-1

Simply put, a balance sheet is a list of everything a company owns and everything it owes. This gives shareholders a snapshot of the company's finances. The best way to study a balance sheet is to compare it to the balance sheets of other companies in the same industry. In addition, you should look at the balance sheet for previous years to get a better idea of where the company has been and where it might be going.

As long as the company is not hiding debt or liabilities, the balance sheet gives you a glimpse of its financial condition. However, reading a balance sheet takes skill because some companies are clever at hiding their expenses and debt while exaggerating their earnings. For example, only a handful of knowledgeable investors figured out that the balance sheets of companies like Enron and WorldCom didn't add up. As it turned out, upper management at these two companies gave an extremely distorted view of the true financial picture. It would have been difficult, if not impossible, for investors to uncover the truth. Nevertheless, before Enron's collapse, financial expert Warren Buffett reminded investors he never invested in a company in which he didn't understand how they made money. The lesson: If you're still confused after reading the balance sheet, invest your money elsewhere.

The Annual Report

For many people, there isn't anything more boring than reading the annual report, a financial report of large, publicly owned corporations. These reports are often long, generally 30 or more pages containing important financial statements such as the balance sheet and income statement. In addition, there might be a letter from the CEO about the steps he or she is taking to make the business more profitable, how the company has performed, and business strategies. Unless you are an accountant or lawyer, it could easily take you all day to wade through the entire report, which often contains public relations fluff. Many pros have learned to focus only on the information in the report they believe is important and ignore the rest.

To cover themselves, many companies will mention all of the risks you'll take if you invest in the company. They also tend to highlight the positive aspects of their business while minimizing the negative. As mentioned before, a few companies purposely deceived investors into believing they were more profitable than they were, although a careful read of the annual report could provide clues that the company was not entirely truthful. Some of the most fascinating tidbits can be found in the footnotes. This is perhaps where you'll learn about perceived risks, ongoing legal issues, and other unforeseen problems.

Although it might be painful to read the entire annual report, it's worth your while to understand where you are putting your hard-earned money. If you are a long-term investor, you want to learn whether or not the company is making money, whether its debt is rising or falling, and if management has a successful business plan.

In the next chapter, you will learn the tools and tactics that fundamental analysts use to value stocks.

10

Fundamental Analysis: Tools and Tactics

Fundamental analysts use a number of tools to evaluate and measure stocks. After all, before you buy a stock, you want to be sure that the company is of good quality and that it is a good value at the price. Investors who primarily use fundamental analysis to choose stocks typically use a variety of tools to decide which stocks to pick. In this section, I briefly describe some of the most popular.

Income Statement: Learning How a Company Makes Money

One of the best ways to determine how much money a company is making is by looking at its *income statement*. This contains a lot of useful information, such as the company's sales, operating expenses, and earnings. Figure 10-1 gives the income statement for Florida Star.

The top line of the income statement gives the company's sales or revenue (also referred to as the *top line*). Look to see if the company's

Florida Star Consolidated Income Statement
    (in thousands)

	2002	2001	2000
SALES REVENUES			
Net Sales	2,895	2,682	1,654
Services	1,764	1,456	789
Hardware	1,591	1,101	961
Software	897	763	690
Total Sales Revenue:	7,147	6,002	4,094
OPERATING EXPENSES			
Cost of sales	2,324	2,643	1,477
Advertising and promotion	987	877	654
Research and Development	104	91	58
Other operating expenses	78	65	29
Total Operating Expenses:	3,493	3,676	2,218
Earnings before income tax:	3,654	2,326	1,876
Provision for income tax:	78	67	43
Net Income:	3,576	2,259	1,833
EARNINGS PER SHARE			
Earnings per share			
of common stock	.99	.87	.76

Figure 10-1

revenue is increasing when compared to that in earlier years. For example, if you are a growth investor, look for companies whose revenue is
increasing by 15 percent or more each year.

The next section of the income statement gives operating expenses.
These are the costs of doing business, such as salaries, advertising,
training employees, and buying new computers, to name a few. There is
usually also a line for research and development (R&D), which is the
cost of developing and investing in new products.

The next three sections of the income statement describe the company's income. Have you heard someone say, "What is the bottom
line?" This refers to a company's net income (which happens to be on

the bottom line of the income statement). After paying all expenses, how much money did the company make? This is net income.

Earnings per Share: Determining How Much Money the Company Makes

No matter how good you think a corporation is or how much you love its managers, if the company isn't earning money, eventually its stock price will fall. That's where EPS comes in. You can find it at the bottom of the company's income statement, below net income. (You calculate EPS by dividing a company's after-tax profit by the company's outstanding shares.) You can also find the EPS in the company's quarterly or annual report, on any number of financial Web sites, such as Yahoo! Finance, or in periodicals like *Barron's*, the *Financial Times*, or the *Wall Street Journal*. The financial newspaper *Investor's Business Daily* also ranks the relative strength of EPS on a scale of 1 to 99. Figure 10-2 gives the EPS for IBM.

If a company is earning more money, it obviously should be rewarded with a higher stock price. That's why it's so useful to compare the company's earnings with those of the previous quarter or the previous year to determine if earnings are going up. (Because some companies are

Earnings Per Share: IBM

Earnings Per Share ($) for Fiscal Year Ending December

	2002	2001	2000	1999	1998	1997
1Q	0.68	0.98	0.83	0.77	0.53	0.59
2Q	0.03	1.15	1.06	1.28	0.75	0.73
3Q	0.76	0.90	1.08	0.93	0.78	0.69
4Q	0.59	1.33	1.48	1.12	1.23	1.05
Year	2.06	4.35	4.44	4.12	3.28	3.00

Figure 10-2

seasonal, quarter-to-quarter comparisons may not be as useful as year-to-year comparisons.)

Unfortunately, finding out how much a company really earns is not as easy as it appears. Some CEOs will play a number of accounting tricks to make it appear that earnings are stronger than they really are. (To keep stock prices artificially high, some CEOs "cooked the books," or changed the numbers so it appeared that the company was making more money than it had in the past. In such cases, when the truth comes out, the company is often forced to restate its earnings, causing the stock to plummet. For example, WorldCom restated its earnings by billions of dollars.)

It's not enough to buy stocks in companies that grow by more than 15 percent a year—you must also understand how the company makes that money. It sometimes takes a stock detective to find out the truth.

The Earnings Estimates Game

Adding to the confusion about EPS, *stock analysts* (people who are paid to independently research corporations and make buy or sell recommendations on their stocks) make estimates or predictions of companies' future earnings. Often, a stock will rise on the expectation that the company's earnings will grow in the future. If a company beats analysts' estimates, the stock price usually goes up. If a company misses analysts' estimates, even by as little as a penny, the stock price usually falls. Sometimes a company will beat analysts' published estimates but not beat the "whisper number," an unofficial earnings estimate that is generally not made public. As noted earlier, CEOs are under extreme pressure to beat the earnings estimates.

Looking at Stock Ratios

The Price/Earnings Ratio: The Granddaddy of Stock Ratios

Many people use the price/earnings ratio (P/E) to get a quick indication of whether the stock price is reasonable given the company's earnings. When you divide the stock price by the company's earnings per share, you end up with a P/E ratio (also known as the *multiple*), that can help you determine whether a stock is fairly valued. Many people think that the P/E is the most effective way to measure a stock. Actually, the P/E is just one of many tools you can use to decide what stocks to buy.

For example, a stock that sells for $20 a share and earned $2 last year has a *trailing* P/E of 10 ($20 divided by $2); the trailing P/E uses earnings from the last year. If a $20 stock were expected to earn $4 next year, it would have a *forward* P/E of 5 ($20 divided by $4). In this case, you are using analysts' estimates concerning what will happen in the future. The great thing about the P/E is that you can easily and quickly compare individual stocks with one another, with their sector, or with the overall market.

Many investors decide whether to buy a stock based on its P/E. For example, *value investors* (bargain hunters looking for stocks of high-quality companies that are selling for a reasonable price) prefer to buy stocks with low P/Es, ideally under 15. (Warren Buffett, for example, buys only companies with trailing P/Es of 10 or less.) On the other hand, *growth investors* (aggressive buyers looking for stocks in companies whose sales or earnings are growing rapidly) don't mind buying stocks with high P/Es because they expect the companies' earnings to improve in the future. If a stock has a P/E of 50 but is growing by 60 percent a year, the stock could be a bargain.

Nevertheless, basing your stock decisions on what a company's earnings might be in the future has backfired on many investors. In particular, analysts' expectations concerning future earnings have often been overly optimistic. For example, in the late 1990s, analyst Mary Meeker continually urged investors to buy shares of Priceline, even though its P/E was outrageously high (it had no earnings and an extremely high stock price). She claimed that traditional fundamental measurements like P/E didn't matter anymore. That was a few months before Priceline fell from hundreds of dollars per share to a couple of dollars. The lesson: P/Es do matter.

Even now, misconceptions about the P/E are common. Just because a stock's P/E is low doesn't mean that you should buy the stock. And just because the P/E is high doesn't mean that the stock should be avoided (although the risk is higher). In general, you can use the P/E to determine quickly if a stock is cheap or expensive when compared with its peers and the overall market. (By the way, pay attention to the P/E of the entire market. For years, the P/E of the S&P 500 was hovering above 30, a clue that the market was overvalued. Some analysts believe that the S&P 500 will have to drop to a P/E of 15, its historical average, before it will be fairly priced.)

Price/Earnings/Growth: Taking the P/E One Step Farther

The P/E ratio is quite useful, but it doesn't take into account future earnings potential. That's what the price/earnings/growth (PEG) ratio is designed to do. To calculate the PEG, instead of simply dividing the stock price by the earnings (as you do for the P/E), you divide the P/E by the earnings growth of the company. For example, if a company has a P/E of 20 and an annual earnings growth rate of 10 percent, the PEG will be 2. This allows you to take into account both the P/E and the company's growth rate in determining the value of a company. Many people feel that the PEG is more accurate than the P/E because it takes future growth into account.

The guideline for PEG users is as follows:

A stock with a PEG of less than 0.50 is desirable (undervalued).

A stock with a PEG between 0.50 and 1 is good (fair value).

A stock with a PEG higher than 1 is not recommended, especially if the PEG is over 2 (overvalued).

Warning: You should use the PEG as only one piece of a larger calculation. Do not decide to buy a stock based solely on its PEG results. For the most complete and accurate calculation, it is suggested that you use the PEG to compare stocks within the same industry. The problem with the PEG, like that with the forward P/E, is that you are basing your information on earnings estimates, which have historically been unreliable. That is why it is so important that you use a variety of tools before deciding to buy or sell a stock.

Price-to-Sales Ratio: Effective for Uncovering Revenue

Because P/E ratios are generally useless with companies that have no earnings, some investors use the price-to-sales ratio (P/S) to decide whether to buy a stock. The reasoning is that although you can play with earnings, you can't play with revenue. With the P/S ratio, you compare price to sales revenue. To calculate the price-to-sales ratio, you divide the company's market capitalization by the total sales revenue booked for the previous year. Some people claim that the P/S is more reliable than the P/E or the PEG. (By the way, before Enron filed for bankruptcy, its P/S ratio reportedly rose to over 200! Typically, a P/S of over 5 is considered high, so 200 was a clear warning sign. It basically meant that investors were paying $200 for each dollar of Enron's sales.) Many value investors will look for stocks with a P/S ratio of less than 1.

Return on Equity: Measuring the Financial Health of a Company

Return on equity (ROE) is a tool that helps you to measure how effectively the company is being managed. Some people consider ROE one of the most important measures of a company's overall financial performance. (You calculate ROE by dividing net income by net worth, although this ratio is not as clear-cut because you must rely on subjective variables to calculate manager efficiency.

In general, the higher the ROE, the more effective the company is at using its resources and the more productive the management team. In other words, ROE gives you an idea of how well the company is managed. The goal is to look for companies with a rising ROE, greater than 15 percent and growing.

There are many other fundamental stock measurements, including return on investment (ROI), debt-to-equity ratio, price-to-book ratio (PB), and return on assets (ROA). The purpose of many of these fundamental tools is to determine whether a stock is a good value compared to its price. Because this is an introductory book, my review of fundamental analysis ends here. For a more thorough examination of fundamental analysis, you'll find dozens of books about this topic at the bookstore or public library.

Problems with Fundamental Analysis

One of the problems with fundamental analysis is that you must rely on the information that a corporation provides. If the corporation is fudging the numbers or is not entirely truthful, then the future earnings projections will be off base. As you know from the recent corporate scandals, many companies, to prop up their stock price, were pressing their accountants and banks to misrepresent expenses as income.

Some corporations were spending money or making loans to executives, but classifying these as income. And in a few cases, CEOs were lying about the numbers. If a corporation gives out overly optimistic earnings numbers or lies, then fundamental analysis by itself won't help you. You need the skill and knowledge of an accomplished accountant to uncover accounting irregularities.

Another problem is that you are making assumptions about a company's future prospects that are hard to prove. Furthermore, fundamental analysis doesn't take into account the psychological reasons that people drive stock prices up. For example, even though the fundamentals showed that many stocks were overpriced during the 1990s, this didn't stop them from going obscenely higher.

A final problem with fundamental analysis is that it is extremely time-consuming. Most individual investors don't take the time or have the knowledge to correctly value a company. Professional money managers hire teams of analysts to do fundamental research on individual companies before they make a stock purchase. Individual investors have to rely on biased research that is passed down from Wall Street or by word of mouth on the Internet.

Biography of Warren Buffett

If you ask professional investors to name the greatest investor of all time, most of them will probably name billionaire Warren Buffett. He is best known as the CEO of $70,000-a-share Berkshire Hathaway, a company involved in a number of businesses, including insurance, publishing, and manufacturing.

Benjamin Graham, the author of two value investment classics, *Security Analysis,* first published in 1934, and *Intelligent Investor,* influenced Buffett early in his life. Buffett later worked for Graham at Graham's brokerage firm, learning from the master how to manage investment portfolios and pick value stocks.

Buffett made a number of successful modifications to Graham's original strategies. He uses a stock's book value, P/E, and dividend yield, among other objective measurements, to calculate the company's fair value. He believes in buying a company for less than it's worth and patiently holding its stock for a lifetime.

One of the reasons Buffett avoided investing in Internet stocks was that he couldn't determine their true value. Buffett strongly believes in buying stocks in companies that are simple and understandable (so that he can calculate their future earnings growth). Most Internet companies had little or no earnings and sky-high P/E ratios. At the time, several pros derided Buffett for avoiding investments in technology companies. In hindsight, Buffett was right.

Buffett has earned a reputation for honesty and a sense of humor. He was one of the first to point out that you should be cautious about investing in companies that play accounting games when they use stock options to compensate employees.

Many people have tried to emulate Buffett's successful buy-and-hold strategies. A number of excellent books have been written about his strategies, most of which are based on common sense. The difficult part for most investors is learning how to value a business—something that Buffett has learned how to do after a lifetime of investment success.

In the next chapter, you will learn how traders use technical analysis to buy and sell stocks.

11

Let's Get Technical: Introduction to Technical Analysis

The ironic thing about technical analysis is that it's sometimes not technical at all. In fact, some people believe that technical analysis is easier to understand than fundamental analysis (although not at first). Have you ever heard the saying that one picture is worth a thousand words? If you have, then you'll appreciate technical analysis because it relies on charts and graphs to help you determine what stocks to buy or sell. When you rely on mechanical tools like *indicators* and *oscillators,* you will be less inclined to trade on the basis of emotion.

Technical analysis is also used to forecast what could happen in the future. By looking at how stocks have reacted in the past, you can make assumptions about what they might do in the future. The shorter the time frame, the more accurate your prediction can be. [Winston Churchill once said, "The farther backward you can look, the farther forward you can see." Quoted by James C. Humes, *Churchill: Speaker of the Century* (Scarborough Books, New York, 1982).]

As you know, fundamental analysis is the study of the data that affect a company. Technical analysis, on the other hand, is the study of the stock price. Short-term traders primarily use technical analysis to help them make buying and selling decisions, although some savvy traders also use fundamental analysis. Conversely, it might help the portfolios of many investors if they double-checked their stock picks using technical analysis.

Nevertheless, keep in mind that technical indicators and charts are simply tools—there is no guarantee that you will be profitable, no matter what method you use or how sophisticated your software or equipment. It really depends on how much effort you put into understanding these stock-picking methods.

The Stock Chart

The key to technical analysis is the stock chart. *Technical analysts,* as they are called, believe that looking at a stock chart is similar to a surgeon's looking at x-rays before operating on a patient. Although charts are not perfect, in the hands of a skilled technician they do provide important clues as to when people are buying or selling. You can use them to help you make statistical assumptions about a stock, or at the very least, to improve the odds that the trade you make will be successful. By reading a stock chart, you can receive clues about how the market will behave in the future and when you should buy or sell.

One of the best reasons for looking at a chart is that it keeps your emotions out of the decision-making process. You may love the company and its CEO, but if the chart shows that the stock is weak and is headed down, you'll probably want to avoid buying it. The good news is that it's easy to find a stock chart on any company you're interested in. Every financial television program—CNBC, Bloomberg, and CNNfn, to name a few—and most financial newspapers, show stock charts. The media discovered a long time ago that one of the easiest ways to show the public how a stock has performed is to display a chart.

The first decision you make when looking at a chart is which time frame you'd like to see. You can select a short time frame—for example, minutes, hours, or a daily chart. Others prefer a longer time frame—

weeks, months, or years. Some traders look at several charts at once, each with a different time frame.

Line, Bar, and Candlestick Charts

Line Charts

A line chart basically plots the closing prices of a stock over a specific period. A line connects the price points. Although line charts are easy to read and understand, they are not as popular with experienced short-term traders because they don't provide very much information. They are most useful when they are combined with other technical indicators. However, many newspapers and television programs use line charts because they are so visually appealing. Figure 11-1 is an example of a line chart.

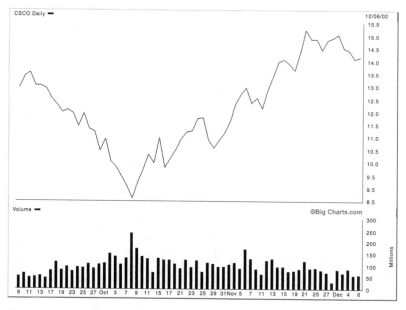

Figure 11-1   Line chart

In this example, you can see immediately that the stock is moving higher. The volume bars are on the bottom. Notice that during the week of October 3, Cisco fell by several points. On October 8, however, there was a spike in volume, and the stock then began to move higher over the next few weeks. More than likely, a large institution *accumulated* (bought) shares of the stock.

Bar Charts

Bar charts are popular with some short-term traders because they are so simple to use and understand. Figure 11-2 is an example of a bar chart. The horizontal scale at the bottom of the chart indicates the specific period (in Figure 11-2, a day). The vertical scale displays the prices the stock can take on during the period. The bar is the range of prices for the period. For example, the top of the bar represents the highest price for the day, and the bottom represents the lowest price for the day. There are also two "ticks" attached to the bar, one that extends to the left and

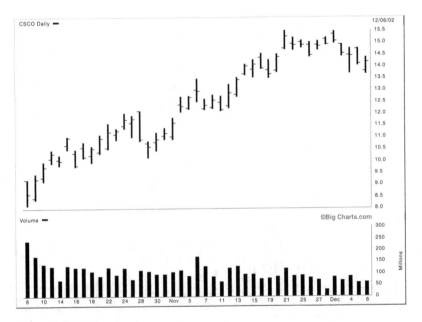

Figure 11-2   Bar chart

one that extends to the right. The left tick stands for the opening price for the trading day, and the right tic marks the closing price.

You can see at a glance, whether the stock closed above or below its opening price. Generally, it is a good sign if a stock closes the day above where it started, especially if there is strong volume right into the close.

Candlestick Charts

Candlestick charts are popular with many traders because they show so much information, including the psychology of the market at any given time. Many traders believe that understanding the emotions of the market is helpful in determining future trends. (A 17th-century rice broker in Japan created the candlestick chart to help him trade rice. As it turned out, his charting methods enabled him to make a fortune in the Japanese rice markets.)

Figure 11-3 is an example of a Candlestick chart. As you can see, candlestick charts use two-dimensional bodies to show the range between the opening and closing prices of a stock during any period. The high and low prices are plotted as single lines and are referred to as wicks (or shadows). The price range between the open and the close is plotted as a narrow rectangle and is referred to as the body. If the stock price ended the day above the opening price, the body of the rectangle is white or clear. If the stock price ended the day below the opening price, the body is black or solid.

Trend Lines

You could say that one of the main purposes of charting is to spot a trend in its early stages. A trend is simply the direction in which a stock is moving over a specific period. A stock usually doesn't move in a straight line, which is why spotting the trend direction is so important.

There are actually three types of trends: *uptrend, downtrend,* and *sideways trend.* The goal is to participate in uptrends while avoiding downtrends. A saying that technicians repeat is, "The trend is your friend (until it ends)." The idea is to ride a trend for as long as possible until it runs out of steam.

Figure 11-3   Candlestick chart

Downtrend

A stock that is in a downtrend is moving lower and has been for a
while. To create a downtrend, draw a line along the top of the chart in
such a way that you connect at least two points. If a stock is in a downtrend with high volume (meaning that a lot of people are selling), the
stock could be in trouble. Figure 11-4 shows an example of a stock in
a downtrend.

If a stock is in a downtrend and has been for a while, you have to be
pretty brave to buy the stock. A few years ago, people used to buy
stocks when they were in a downtrend because they assumed that the
trend was only temporary. This aggressive strategy actually worked
until the 2000 bear market arrived. At that point, instead of there being
a temporary dip, most stocks kept going down, wiping out the accounts
of many investors. No matter what you think of technical analysis, it is
a mistake to ignore what you see on a stock chart.

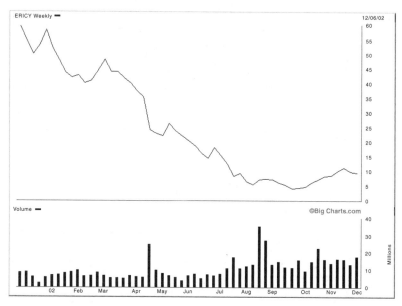

Figure 11-4   Downtrend

Uptrend

A stock that is moving higher and has been for a while is in an uptrend. To create an uptrend, draw a line along the bottom of the chart in such a way that you connect at least two points. Many short-term traders like to buy stocks that are trending higher. (Instead of buying low and selling high, traders might buy high and sell higher.) Just as in a downtrend, traders will look at volume to help determine whether the stock is a good buy. After all, if a stock is moving higher on increasing volume, a lot of people are buying it. Figure 11-5 shows a stock index in an uptrend.

Figure 11-5 is a weekly chart of the Dow Jones Industrial Average. As you can see, although the index didn't move up in a straight line, the trend is still up. This is obviously a very positive sign if you are a buyer. The challenge, of course, is determining how long the uptrend will continue. Given this chart, since there are signs that the uptrend

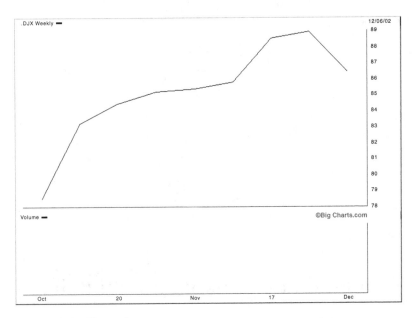

Figure 11-5   Uptrend

has ended at $89, short-term traders may sell their long positions or sell short.

Sideways Trend

There is really nothing more frustrating than watching a stock go up and down but end up in the same place where it began. This is what we call a *sideways trend*. A stock in a sideways trend is moving up and down like a bouncing ball but is so disorganized that it's hard to know which direction it's going. If you are a trader, you generally avoid getting involved with stocks that are trading sideways. By the way, the volume in a sideways pattern is often very low. Figure 11-6 shows a stock in a sideways trend.

Although trading stocks that are in a sideways trend is difficult, sometimes the sweetest profits come when a stock that is trading sideways for a while (traders will say that the stock is *consolidating*) suddenly breaks violently up or down. The difficult part, however, is

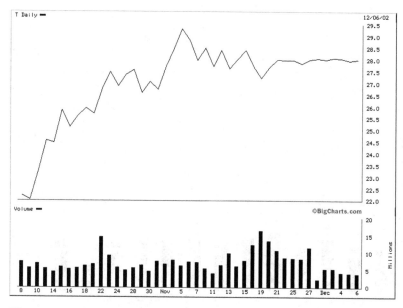

Figure 11-6   Sideways trend

figuring out when the sideways pattern will finally end. It would be dangerous for a short-term trader to buy the stock in Figure 11-6 because it is so unpredictable. It could easily move in either direction.

Trend Reversal

One of the challenges of technical analysis is to determine when the current stock trend will run out of steam and reverse direction. In fact, technicians are constantly on the lookout for the "breaking" of the trend line, which signifies a *trend reversal*. Figure 11-7 gives an example of a stock index that has reversed direction.

In Figure 11-7, the index QQQQ was clearly in a downtrend in early September. By the end of the month, however, it had suddenly reversed direction, and it continued to move higher. A short-term trader isn't especially concerned about why the stock reversed direction—only that it did. Identifying this trend reversal and buying it during the early stages could be very profitable for a trader. In this case, holding the

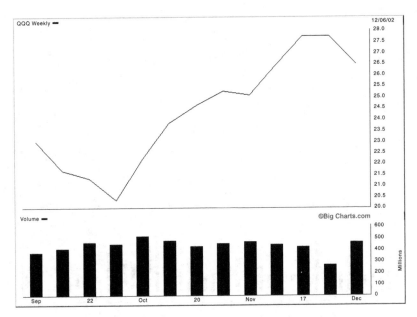

Figure 11-7   Trend reversal

stock for a month or longer (until there was another trend reversal) would have brought the most profits.

The challenge is to identify a trend reversal before it happens. If you do identify a trend reversal, it's essential you use other technical indicators to confirm that it's real and not just a temporary reversal. Also, just because a trend has continued for a long time doesn't mean that it's in any danger of a reversal. Long trend lines are very common.

Support and Resistance

Support: Buyers Win the Battle

If you understand *support* and *resistance,* you will have a better idea of when to buy or sell a stock. Support and resistance keep appearing on stock charts no matter what method of technical analysis you use. If you want to be a successful trader, you will need to understand how to identify support and resistance on a stock chart.

When a stock price is falling, there will be certain places on the way down when buyers will step in and prevent the stock from falling further. Support is the price level at which a stock's price has stopped falling and either is moving sideways or has reversed direction. The demand for the stock is thought to be strong enough to prevent the price from dropping further. The buyers are in control.

Support is often at whole numbers because people tend to buy at whole numbers. When you look at a chart, you can often find support levels by studying how the stock reacted in the past. Let's use the popular 3-month chart given in Figure 11-8 to show support, which is between $56 and $57 a share.

In Figure 11-8, support is at $56.50 a share, the price that Johnson & Johnson (JNJ) hit three times before reversing. In fact, after the period shown in this chart, JNJ couldn't hold either $56.50 or $56, but

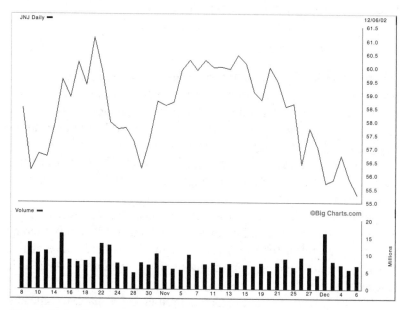

Figure 11-8   Support

continued to fall. In such a case, technicians say that the stock "broke through support." When this happens, it is a very bad sign. It means that there aren't enough buyers to support the stock at that price level. Technicians also notice that this stock is making a series of "lower lows," which means that the support level keeps going lower. At least in the short term, this is not a good sign for the stock.

In the 1990s, one of the most closely followed stocks in the United States was Cisco Systems (CSCO). It seemed as if everyone owned shares in this company. Although the stock was wildly popular, technical analysts paid close attention to its support level, which was $50 a share. Every time Cisco dropped to $50, it bounced back.

In early 2000, Cisco fell below $50 a share, breaking through support. Once this happened, many short-term traders who used technical analysis sold their shares. When all these people sold at once, Cisco headed lower, eventually dropping to a low of $10 a share in 2002. According to technicians, no matter how good the fundamentals or how much you love the stock, when the stock breaks through its support level on increasing volume, it's time to sell.

Resistance: Sellers Win the Battle

When a stock's price is rising, there will be certain places on the way up when sellers step in and prevent the stock from rising further. *Resistance* is the price level at which a stock's price has stopped rising and either is moving sideways or has reversed direction. The stock can't go any higher. This is the point at which people, for whatever reason, sold their shares of stock. The sellers are in control. There isn't enough demand for the stock to rise any higher. An example of resistance is shown in Figure 11-9.

In this example, Boeing (BA) tried to break through resistance at $37 a share through the entire month of September. When this attempt was unsuccessful, it tried to break through $36 a share. Once again, sellers prevented Boeing from going higher. It then retreated until it reached support at $29.

If Boeing had been able to break through $37 a share, technicians would have said that the stock "broke through resistance." This indicates that a stock is strong and can be bought on the way up. It is common for

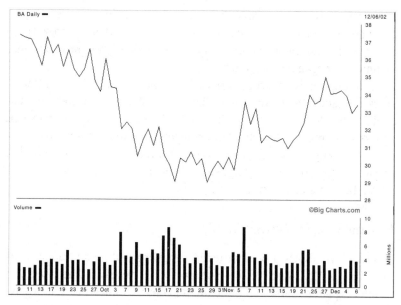

Figure 11-9   Resistance

stocks to break through resistance and go much higher, especially in a bull market. (By the way, many professional traders wait until a stock breaks through support or resistance before making a trade.)

Warning: Although it is possible to find fantastic stock plays using technical analysis, it isn't easy. For instance, a stock might break through resistance and move much higher. Right after you place your buy order, however, the stock suddenly reverses course and drops 5 points! Although technical analysis seems easy on paper or when you read about it in a book, in real life it is harder to master than it seems.

Introduction to Stock Patterns

Technical analysts are constantly searching for stock patterns that will give them clues to what might happen in the future. One reason you repeatedly see the same stock patterns is that people tend to make the same mistakes—for example, buying high and selling low. Stock patterns are one tool that technicians use to evaluate what the crowds are doing. In fact, so many patterns showed up regularly on the charts that technicians began naming them.

Although these chart patterns will not absolutely tell you where a stock is headed, there are signals that technicians look for to help them decide when to buy or sell. In the hands of an expert, identifying stock patterns can prevent disaster. Unfortunately, not many people can successfully recognize stock patterns until it's too late. Nevertheless, that shouldn't stop you from trying, since some patterns are so obvious that even a beginner can identify them in their early stages.

Head and Shoulders Pattern (Bearish)

Figure 11-10 shows a bearish reversal pattern that many traders consider one of the most reliable and profitable patterns. The head and shoulders pattern shows up quite often in charts, indicating that buying

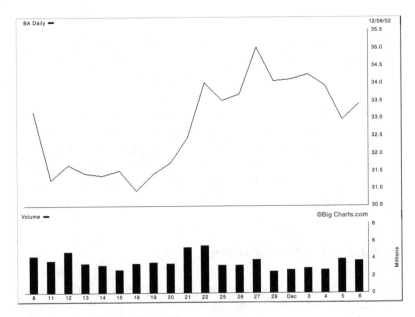

Figure 11-10   Head and shoulders pattern

has stopped at the top of the trend, and it is about to reverse direction. Notice the head and the right and left shoulders. The point where the shoulders meet is the neckline.

Analysis: The stock moves higher but pulls back to form the left shoulder. It then moves higher to form the head, which seems bullish. It then falls back to its support level or neckline, which is the alignment of the two support levels. The stock rises again to form the right shoulder but fails to break resistance. Keep your eye on the neckline, because the stock is doomed in the short term if it breaks below the neckline (which it did in Figure 11-10). The broken neckline confirms that the upward trend of the stock has been reversed.

Reverse Head and Shoulders Pattern (Bullish)

Unlike the bearish head and shoulders pattern, the reverse head and shoulders is bullish. It is a mirror image of a head and shoulders pattern and shows that a bottom has been reached. In Figure 11-11, because the

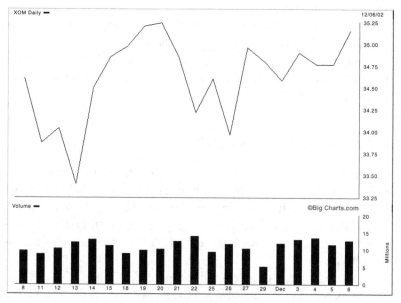

Figure 11-11   Reverse head and shoulders pattern

stock moved strongly past the neckline on rising volume, it's a good time to buy.

Analysis: The stock drops to $34.25, then reverses direction to form an inverted left shoulder. It then rallies until it hits resistance and retreats, forming the head at $34. Once again, the stock rises to resistance and falls to $34.50, where it forms the inverted right shoulder. The stock then retreats briefly but reverses direction, breaking through resistance and advancing strongly. Once it breaks the neckline, the stock is temporarily unstoppable.

Double Top (Bearish—Looks Like an M)

The double top is a common bearish pattern that shows two peaks at the same price level. The stock has twice failed to break through the resistance level; this indicates that you should switch from buying on the upside to selling. When the stock tries to break through the top of the second leg, it will probably fail and sell off. The stock could consolidate for weeks or months before breaking down. Figure 11-12 is an example of a double top.

In this example, the stock falls sharply after twice failing to break resistance at $19.25 a share, forming the double top. Notice that a very bearish *triple top* has been formed at $18.75, setting this stock up for a short-term fall. If you were a technician, you would sell your long position or sell this stock short.

Double Bottom (Bullish—Looks Like a W)

The double bottom is a very common bullish reverse pattern. The stock has failed to break through key support levels, indicating that you could switch from selling on the downside to buying on the upside. The stock could consolidate for weeks or months before breaking out to the upside, however. Figure 11-13 is an example of a double bottom.

In the example, Coca-Cola falls to its support level of $44.90. The bulls think they are in control when the stock temporarily rises before

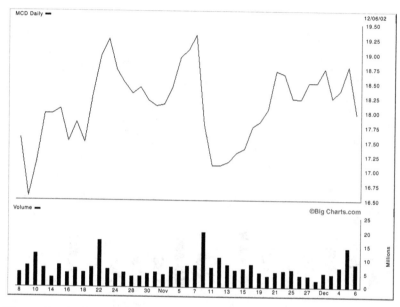

Figure 11-12   Double top

retreating to $44.90 a second time. Once again, support holds and the stock reverses direction. This time, however, Coca-Cola zooms past resistance and never looks back until it hits $45.50 a share. (By the way, if the stock retreats and holds support for a third time at $44.90, it would make a triple bottom, an extremely bullish stock pattern.

How Chart Patterns Could Have Saved Your Portfolio

If you look closely at the 4-year chart of the Nasdaq in Figure 11-14, you will see two obvious patterns: a head and shoulders in April 2000 followed by a double top. Knowledgeable technical analysts who saw these patterns should have seen a disaster looming! (In fact, many technical analysts missed or didn't believe the signals. However, an extremely profitable trader friend of mine who saw the head and shoul-

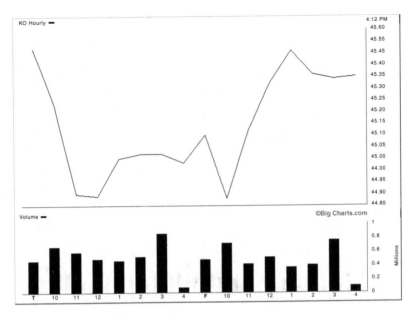

Figure 11-13   Double bottom

ders formation immediately warned me, in April 2000, to sell all my stocks and mutual funds.)

In the above example, you can see the Nasdaq topping out in March 2000. It formed a head and shoulders pattern (as well as a double top), falling back to its neckline before breaking support near 4500 and eventually falling to 3500, where it temporarily held support. Many technicians (as well as many fundamental analysts) incorrectly called a market bottom.

The Nasdaq formed a clear-cut double top pattern at 4200 but couldn't break resistance. This gave observant traders a second chance to get out of the market. After failing to break 4200, it reversed direction, breaking support levels and making a series of lower lows. By now, the Nasdaq was doomed. Alert traders bailed out or, even better, sold short. You can see on the chart how many times the Nasdaq rallied, only to fall further when the rally failed. These false rallies (called *head fakes*) can fool even many professional traders. In retrospect, it's

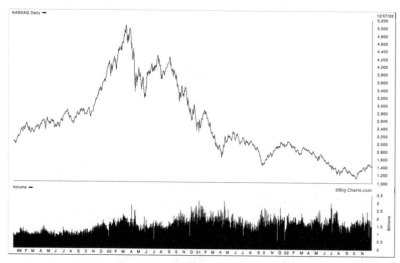

Figure 11-14   Nasdaq head and shoulders

easy to see the stock patterns, but in the heat of battle they are not that obvious.

Gaps

Gaps are simply open spaces in the stock pattern. For whatever reason (perhaps breaking news in the middle of the night), there was no trading at a particular price level and the stock jumps—there is an order imbalance between buy and sell orders. Gaps are significant because they indicate strong buying or selling demand. Figure 11-15 shows an example of a gap.

In Figure 11-15, notice the gap or open space between the first Tuesday closing price at 4:00 p.m. and the first Wednesday opening price at 9:30 a.m. On the Wednesday opening, IBM is said to have "gapped up" from its $85 closing price to $86 with no trades in between. Notice the strong volume in the stock on the gap up. In the short term, probably because of positive news that was released after the market closed, buy-

Figure 11-15   Gaps

ers overwhelmed sellers, causing IBM to gap up. Notice that there was another gap up between Friday and Monday. Unfortunately, what goes up sometimes comes down. There is a noticeable 2-point "gap down" at the market opening on the second Wednesday.

Technicians have identified three types of gaps: continuation, breakaway, and exhaustion.

1. *The breakaway gap.* This shows a stock gapping up strongly on high volume. The stock will make a series of new highs. (Technicians love to join breakaway gaps because they are so powerful.)

2. *The continuation gap.* This is similar to the breakaway gap except that it occurs in the middle of a price trend, not at the beginning. It's possible that the stock will continue to make a strong move in the same direction, just as with the breakaway gap. Figure 11-15 shows a continuation gap.

3. *The exhaustion gap.* This shows a stock that gaps up or down but doesn't reach new highs or lows. As a result, it is likely that the price move will fail (or be exhausted), and the stock will immediately return to *fill the gap* (retreat to the earlier price). If you identify an exhaustion gap, get out as quickly as you can.

Some short-term traders are skilled at playing gaps. For example, if you were fast, you could have bought IBM on the market opening at $86 a share and sold it a few minutes later at $88, for a 2-point gain. This is the kind of play that short-term traders live for. Unfortunately, many stocks will gap up or down and suddenly reverse direction to fill the gap. Keep in mind that trading on the basis of gaps is a difficult maneuver that takes a lot of practice if it is to be successful.

For example, suppose that when the market opens for trading, the S&P or the Dow index has gapped up (or down) substantially from its previous close. Skilled technicians will "buy the gap up" but keep a tight stop. Others will "fade the gap," or trade in the opposite direction from the gap.

As mentioned in an earlier chapter, if you are a first-time trader, it's best to avoid making trades as soon as the market opens. This is when professional traders dominate the market playing field, using large sums of money to move stocks in one direction or the other. Making trades based on gaps is best left to the professionals.

Problems with Technical Analysis

Critics of technical analysis claim that reading stock charts is similar to telling your fortune using tea leaves. They claim that it's impossible to make predictions about the future based on what happened in the past. Tomorrow is all that matters, according to the critics. In addition, critics claim that there is no proof that technical analysis actually works. Perhaps the only way to find out for sure is to try it for yourself. Just like fundamental analysis, technical analysis is as much an art as a science. It takes an extremely competent and dedicated technician to find good stock picks using technical analysis.

Biography of Jesse Livermore

One of the best known and most successful traders was Jesse Livermore. While still a teenager, he quit school to become a "board boy" for a stock brokerage firm. (Before computers were invented, board boys updated stock and bond prices on a large chalkboard.)

The story of Jesse Livermore's life and the lessons he learned about trading can be found in his book, *Reminiscences of a Stock Operator,* originally published in 1923. Although the author is given as Edwin Lefevre, many believe that Livermore wrote the book himself. It is still one of the most popular and valuable books ever written on speculating in the stock market.

Livermore spent much of his time trading in "bucket shops." (Bucket shops are unlicensed brokerages; they have been described as "gambling dens.") He was so successful at trading stocks that he was banned from most bucket shops. He was forced to wear disguises and use fake names in order to trade. Nevertheless, this gave him the opportunity to watch how other traders manipulated the markets. After closely studying the markets, he created a successful rule-based trading system. As he became wealthier, Livermore made most of his trades from an elaborate secret office that was connected by telephone to the New York Stock Exchange.

Much of the money that Livermore made came from shorting stocks (he was famously bearish). He made a lot of enemies on his roller-coaster ride, and he was often opposed by some of the country's most influential financial leaders. Keep in mind that many of the tactics that Livermore used are now illegal, including manipulating stocks by using inside information and arranging with reporters to have incorrect information published. (One of his tricks was to wait until he had made a profit on a stock, then reveal to an influential reporter that a particular stock was a great buy. When the stock went higher, he immediately unloaded his position.)

Not long after making and losing his fourth million-dollar fortune, Livermore walked into a hotel hat check room and shot himself in the head. Although he had once been worth millions, dated glamorous actresses, and owned a number of houses and boats, at the time of his death at age 63 his estate was reported to be worth less than $10,000.

In the next chapter, you will learn the tools and tactics that technical analysts use to evaluate stocks.

12

Technical Analysis: Tools and Tactics

Just as with fundamental analysis, there are tools that technical analysts use to determine when to buy or sell a stock. All of the tools explained in this chapter can be found on a stock chart (since technicians study stock prices using charts). By the time you finish this chapter, you should have a better understanding of many of the tools and tactics used by technical analysts. For some people, technical analysis can seem confusing. With practice, however, it should make more sense.

Volume: An Underestimated but Powerful Indicator

Volume shows how many shares changed hands during a given period. It is the fuel that drives stock prices higher or lower. By studying the volume of shares being traded, you can obtain clues as to whether a stock is moving because of true buying or selling interest or other factors that could influence the direction of the stock.

In today's market, billions of shares of stock are traded every day on all three stock exchanges. If less than a billion shares are traded during the day, it is considered a light volume day. It isn't hard to guess why this is true. In 1929, only 8 percent of the people in the United States were invested in the stock market. Now it is estimated that over 60 percent of the people are invested in the market, either through mutual funds or directly in stocks.

Sometimes you will hear people on Wall Street talk about a liquid market. This is another way of saying that there is a lot of volume in the market or in an individual stock. The pros on Wall Street want to see a lot of liquidity and do everything in their power to bring people into the market, especially buyers. The more liquid a stock is, the easier it is to get into and out of it. That is why you want a lot of liquidity in the market.

Advanced Technical Indicators and Oscillators

Now I'm going to show you a couple of neat little tools, called *technical indicators and oscillators,* that short-term traders use before they enter or exit a trade. Although there are dozens of these technical indicators, we'll look at the most popular. Be aware that it takes a while to thoroughly understand many of these tools.

Moving Averages: Simple but Powerful Tools

One of the simplest but most valuable technical indicators for both investors and traders is the *moving average* (MA). A moving average is the average price of a stock for a specified period—for example, a specified number of hours, days, or weeks. When plotted on a chart, it is displayed as a line that moves forward with each trading day. When moving averages are put on a chart, they give technicians a lot of clues about where a stock is headed.

Many technical analysts use moving averages as support and resistance. If the stock price rises above the moving average, this is seen as a bullish sign. Conversely, if the stock price drops below the moving average, this is seen as bearish and is a signal to sell. In particular, many institutional investors use the 200-day MA as support and resistance. For example, if the stock price is trading below the 200-day MA, this is a signal to sell. If the stock price is trading above the 200-day MA, this is a signal to buy.

Short-term traders tend to use the 40- or 50-day MA to determine support and resistance levels. It's sometimes uncanny how a stock can nudge up to the 40- or 50-day MA and then immediately reverse direction. Keep in mind that you should not base your trading decisions solely on moving averages (or any other technical indicator), but the MA does give you an idea of the strength and direction of the stock trend. Figure 12-1 shows a stock chart with two moving averages—the 50-day MA and the 200-day MA.

In Figure 12-1, for much of the period shown, Caterpillar remained well below its 50-day and 200-day MA. Near the end of August, it bumped up against the 50-day MA before reversing direction. At the end of October, the stock broke through the 50-day MA on rising volume, a very positive sign. By the end of November, it also broke through the 200-day MA. From a short-term technical perspective, this stock should be held until there are signs that it has run out of steam.

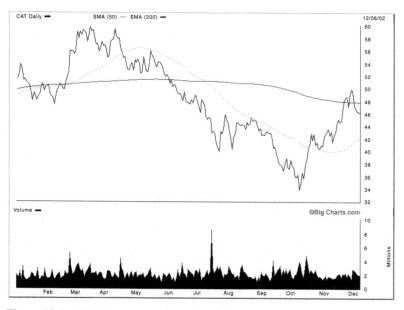

Figure 12-1   Moving averages

On-Balance Volume (OBV): A Measure of Volume

On-balance volume (OBV) is one of the most underutilized but important indicators. OBV measures volume, which, as you remember, is the force that makes stocks go up or down. When you put OBV on a chart, a volume line appears at the bottom of the chart on top of the volume bars. OBV basically measures how much money is flowing into or out of a security.

If the OBV line is dropping, it tells you that people are selling. If the OBV line is rising, it tells you that people are buying. After all, no matter what is happening in the market, if people are pulling money out of a stock, its price will go down. Conversely, if people are buying a stock, its price will go up. Figure 12-2 gives an example of OBV.

Because technical analysis is not an exact science, many traders use OBV to confirm what is happening with a stock. For example, let's say that a stock is up by 3 points but the OBV is dropping. This tells you that although the stock is temporarily going up, it's not going to last.

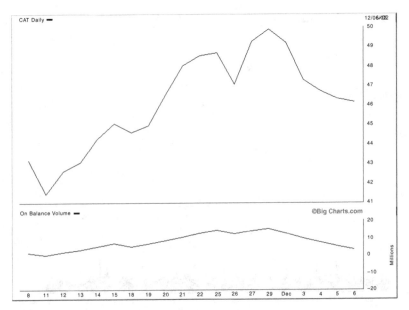

Figure 12.2   On-balance volume

For whatever reason, people, most likely institutional investors, are selling. The dropping OBV is a signal that you should immediately sell the stock. In Figure 12-2, the OBV initially rose along with the Caterpillar stock price. In early December, the OBV was slowly dropping along with the Caterpillar stock price. This was a clear signal that, at least for the short term, institutional investors were selling this stock.

One of the biggest problems with technical analysis is that you sometimes get false signals. OBV helps you determine whether the buying and selling pressure is real or whether a reversal is imminent. For example, let's say that the price of a stock is falling but OBV is rising. An alert trader will buy, not sell, because it's possible that the stock price will reverse as more buyers accumulate shares.

Relative Strength Indicator: A Measure of Whether Stocks Are Overbought or Oversold

The relative strength indicator (RSI) measures the relative strength or weakness of a stock when it is compared to itself over a specified period. It is an *oscillator* with an upper and lower band that ranges from 0 to 100 on a vertical scale. An example of the RSI is given in Figure 12-3.

To understand the RSI, you need to know what is meant by *relative strength* and *relative weakness,* two of the most important concepts in technical analysis. Relative strength means that a stock is strong compared to another stock or to an index. For example, if the Nasdaq is falling but Bright Light is rising, then Bright Light is strong relative to the Nasdaq. (From a technical viewpoint, stocks with relative strength are good buys.) Conversely, if the Nasdaq is going up but Bright Light is dropping in price, then Bright Light has relative weakness. (Generally, you avoid buying stocks with relative weakness.)

When used in conjunction with other technical indicators such as moving averages and OBV, the RSI is a powerful tool that can help to identify whether a stock is *overbought* or *oversold.* This allows you to determine which stocks are going to run out of energy and succumb to the bears (overbought). On the other hand, the RSI will also help you to identify stocks that have fallen and are about to reverse and move higher (oversold).

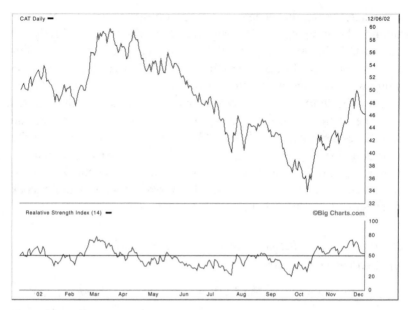

Figure 12-3   Relative strength indicator

For example, if the stock price is dropping, but the RSI rises above 70 and then crosses back down, this is a sign that the stock might reverse direction (this price reversal is called *divergence*). Conversely, if the stock price is rising, but the RSI drops below 30 and crosses back up, the stock might reverse. The idea is that the stock price will eventually move in the direction of the RSI.

In Figure 12-3, the RSI dropped as low as 20 twice in the last year, signaling that Caterpillar might be oversold. For example, in August the RSI fell to 20 and crossed back up, and the stock immediately reversed direction. Then, in October, the RSI again fell to 20 and crossed back up. Note what happened to Caterpillar—the stock reversed its downtrend and began a strong rally that continued for a month.

If you are critical of technical analysis, you can argue that the RSI generated a series of short-term signals, some of which were unclear. This is why it's so important to use the RSI in conjunction with other technical indicators. On the other hand, the RSI did work flawlessly in the end, identifying that Caterpillar was oversold and would eventually reverse its downtrend.

Bollinger Bands: Another Measure of Whether Stocks Are Overbought or Oversold

Like the RSI, Bollinger bands are an *oscillator* that helps traders identify whether a stock is overbought or oversold. Bollinger bands have two lines, an upper and a lower band with a gap between them that expands or contracts as the stock price moves. You should keep your eye on the third line in the middle. This is called the price indicator, and where it goes signals whether a stock is about to reverse direction. An example of Bollinger bands is given in Figure 12-4.

Technicians look for a number of signals when using Bollinger bands. First, if the two outer bands move so close together that they are almost touching (narrow), this is a signal that there could be a sudden move in the stock price, either up or down. Second, if the price indicator

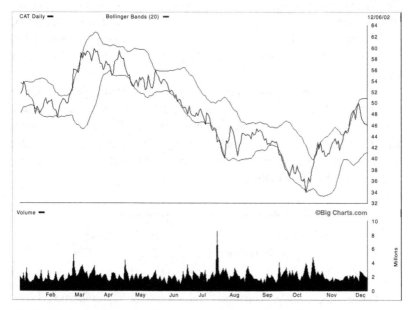

Figure 12-4   Bollinger bands

is pushed well outside the upper or lower band, this means that there is strong buying or selling activity. Many times, a stock will ride the upper or lower band for minutes or hours and then cross through. Often, if the price indicator begins in one band, it will cross to the other band. This tells you that in the next few minutes, or perhaps hours, the stock price will reverse direction.

The good news is that in the hand of an expert, technical indicators like Bollinger bands are extremely useful. The bad news is that the indicators change so quickly that they are useful primarily to short-term traders. As always, you should experiment and practice before risking real money on technical indicators or oscillators.

Conclusion

One of the problems with technical analysis is that it is extremely difficult to read the signals correctly. If all it took to be successful in the market were sophisticated oscillators and indicators, then most people would use only technical analysis. Although most investors should have a basic understanding of how to read charts and how to use technical indicators like moving averages, this probably won't help for long-term investments. After all, technical analysis is most useful for short-term decisions.

Although charting stocks can be fun and profitable, you must also be careful to keep it simple. Many traders find that the more indicators they use on a chart, the more confused they get. It is what one trader friend of mine calls "analysis paralysis." You spend so much time studying charts that you don't make trades. Keep it simple—the less complicated the information on your chart, the better.

Speculating on Commodities and Futures Contracts*

The futures exchanges were created to provide a market for pork bellies, hogs, cattle, corn, and hundreds of other commodities. A futures contract is simply an agreement that requires the holder to buy or sell a commodity at a predetermined price during a specified period of time. For only 10 percent down, you can speculate on commodities for the chance to make a small fortune. It is not uncommon for speculators to make as much as $100,000 or more in a day while risking no more than $10,000.

Although the odds are better than those at gambling, it is estimated that over 95 percent of the people who trade futures lose money—and these are the people who supposedly know what they're doing. In addition, you could easily lose more than what you started with.

At the Chicago Mercantile Exchange (the Merc) in Chicago, Illinois, traders verbally announce the order and price and keep shouting until the order is filled. In addition, they use hand signals to communicate with other traders. To an outsider, it looks like total chaos.

Although directly trading futures is best left to the professionals, there are mutual funds that specialize in future contracts. If trading futures fascinates you, a safer idea is to learn how to trade the *E-minis,* or future contracts of the S&P 500 and the Nasdaq 100. If you do lose money trading the E-minis, at least you won't lose more than you started with.

By looking at the index futures, you can get an idea as to whether the markets will open strong or weak. A number of traders depend on index futures to plan their trades for the day. Hours before the market opens, the traders at the Merc are already buying or selling futures contracts for the Dow, Nasdaq, or S&P 500. If you turn to a financial channel like CNBC, CNNfn, or Bloomberg, you will notice whether the index futures are up or down before the market opens.

---

*Some of the text used in this sidebar originally appeared in my first book, *101 Investment Lessons by the Wizards of Wall Street* (Career Press, 1999).

In the next chapter, you will learn how to use psychology to determine whether to buy or sell a stock.

13

The Psychology of Stocks: Introduction to Sentiment Analysis

Sentiment analysis involves studying psychological clues to help you determine where the market is headed. It is not as clear-cut as fundamental or technical analysis, but it is just as important. Understanding where the crowds (what Wall Street calls the herd) are investing their money will help you decide how to invest. Usually, when you find out where the crowds are investing, you do the opposite!

Sentiment analysts use a number of tools to determine market psychology. For example, when the market was going into the stratosphere, every psychological indicator showed that people were gorging on stocks. The market went up so far so quickly that Alan Greenspan, the Federal Reserve Board chairman, remarked that investors were suffering from "irrational exuberance." He made this comment in 1996, four years before the bull market ended! Although market psychology was telling us that stocks were due for a nasty fall, it took four years before it actually happened.

Psychological Indicators

Nevertheless, there are some important psychological indicators that you should look at if you want to be ready when the market reverses. The following are four psychological indicators that can help you learn where the crowds are investing.

The Chicago Board Options Exchange Volatility Index

The Chicago Board Options Exchange Volatility Index (VIX) is an index that measures the volatility of the U.S. stock market by tracking S&P 100 option contracts. When you use the VIX as a contrarian indicator, the higher the VIX goes (because option buyers are bearish), the more likely it is that the market will reverse and go higher. Conversely, when the VIX goes lower (because option buyers are bullish), it is more likely that the market will go lower. The more extreme the VIX reading, the more likely it is that the market will reverse direction.

It probably seems confusing that if option buyers are bullish, according to the VIX, the market will go lower, and if option buyers are bearish, the market could go higher. The reason is that 90 percent of option traders lose money, so according to this theory, the chances are good that if you do the opposite of what most option traders do, you will do well. That's why the VIX is called a contrarian indicator.

The VIX usually stays in a range between 20 and 30. Historically, when the VIX is well above 30, option traders are bearish (if you look at the stock market, you will notice that the market is going down). Conversely, when the VIX drops below 20, option traders are bullish (the rising market reflects their enthusiasm). Using the VIX as an indicator, when options are too bullish or too bearish, the market is likely to reverse direction. (There's an old saying: When the VIX is low, it's time to go. When the VIX is high, it's time to buy.)

If you look at the chart in Figure 13-1, you'll notice that in early 2000, at the peak of the bull market, the VIX dropped as low as 18 (because option traders believed that the market was going higher). It wasn't long before the market topped out and the economy began a long and slow descent into a bear market.

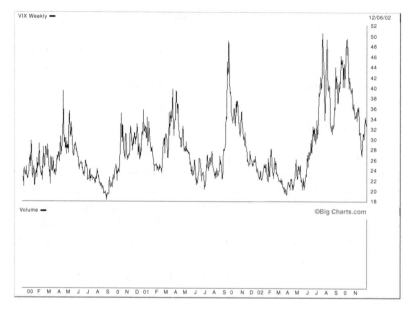

Figure 13-1   VIX

Conversely, right after September 11, 2001, the VIX went as high as 50 as investors panicked because of terrorism concerns. It turned out to be an ideal time to buy stocks, at least in the short term. Like any technical tool, the VIX is by no means foolproof. The VIX often stays at one level for months, giving no clue to what investors are feeling.

The Media

Many people use the media as a contrarian indicator. In other words, by the time something is reported in the media, you better do the opposite. For example, a few years ago, guests appeared on television and on the radio gushing about the "new economy," the unstoppable stock market, and the popularity of the Internet. This was a clear sign that the markets might reverse. After we made it to the new millennium (remember Y2K?) without a stock market crash or a computer meltdown, most people thought that the worst was behind us. Little did they know that, at least from an investment perspective, the worst was yet to come.

For another popular contrarian signal, look in the financial periodical *Barron's* for the Investor's Intelligence reading, which surveys newsletter writers. If newsletter writers are overwhelmingly bullish (over 55 or 60 percent), this is a bearish sign. Conversely, if newsletter writers are overwhelmingly bearish, this is a bullish sign.

Mutual Fund Redemptions

You can learn a lot by keeping an eye out for increased mutual fund redemptions (which means that individual investors are selling their mutual funds). This will give you a clue as to what the crowds are thinking. The financial newspaper *Investor's Business Daily* regularly measures mutual fund redemptions. In addition, the business section of most daily newspapers lets you know what mutual fund investors are doing with their money.

There are two ways to look at increased mutual fund redemptions. On the one hand, it is bearish because if investors are pulling their money out of the market at any price, it will force fund managers to sell shares of the stocks that they hold. On the other hand, it is bullish because it sets the market up for the next phase, capitulation, which creates a market bottom.

Capitulation

Capitulation refers to what happens when everyone in the market panics and immediately sells all of their stocks, causing a stock crash. The theory behind capitulation is that after everyone sells their stocks and mutual funds in a panic, the market hits bottom, with nowhere to go but up. In addition, anyone who has cash comes in to buy unloved stocks at fire-sale prices. If there is capitulation, the markets will fall by huge amounts—10 percent or more in one day.

Investors have capitulated twice in the twentieth century, in 1929 (with the market eventually falling 89 percent from its high) and in 1987 (with the market plummeting by over 20 percent in one day). Nevertheless, it took only a year and a half for the market to recover from the 1987 crash. After the crash of 1929, however, it took 25 years for the market to return to its precrash level. Although the chances are good that investors will again capitulate one day (a dramatic and tragic event that could send people fleeing from the markets), if history is any guide, if you can keep your head and not panic, you will hopefully see this as a buying opportunity.

Stock Market Scams

Since we just finished talking about what could go wrong in the stock market, this is a good time to make you aware of two of the most common stock scams.

The Pump and Dump

The pump and dump is one of the easiest and most common ways of taking money away from unsuspecting investors. Although it is illegal, the use of the pump and dump has actually increased because the Internet has made it possible to reach millions more people. Here's how the pump and dump works.

First, company insiders try to convince outsiders to buy a stock, usually the stock of a small over-the-counter company. Investors are led to believe that this is a "once-in-a-lifetime" opportunity to make a small fortune. The fraudsters will pump up interest in the stock by sending messages through Internet chat rooms, attempting to go on television or radio, or posting overly optimistic press releases. Before the Internet, pump and dumpers used to call people on the telephone. The idea is to artificially pump up the price of a stock by spreading false news. The stock price rises because of increased buying and speculation, not because of anything positive happening in the company.

As the stock goes higher, those with inside knowledge are prepared for the "dump." As more people buy shares of the stock, the insiders sell all their shares for a huge profit. Eventually, the truth comes out, and the stock price falls as more people sell. Guess who is left holding the shares of the now nearly worthless stock? You guessed it—the unsuspecting investors who bought into the hype. They probably thought the price could go higher, so they never sold their shares.

The pump and dump is one of the oldest and most effective scams. Usually, pump and dumps are used on small stocks selling for between $1 and $5 a share because it is easier for pump-and-dumpers to manipulate the stock price with smaller stocks.

Insider Trading

There are actually two types of insider trading: legal and illegal. Legal insider trading is that done by company employees (insiders) who file proper paperwork with the SEC before buying and selling shares in their company. These documents are available for viewing on the SEC Web site.

On the other hand, illegal insider trading occurs when company employees buy and sell stocks based on information that is not known to the public. For example, it's illegal for the managers of Bright Light to buy additional shares of stock in the company if they know that a revolutionary new product is about to be released. It's even illegal for you to buy shares of stock in that situation if company insiders (perhaps your neighbor) tell you about it.

Do you think insider trading is common? It certainly is; it occurs a lot more often than many people think. Every once in a while the SEC catches a celebrity just to make a point that it's watching. Nevertheless, it's my estimate that thousands of insiders are using information gleaned from the companies they work for to make profitable transactions. It's an open secret on Wall Street that those in the know are trading stocks on inside information.

In the next chapter, you will find out why stocks go up or down, which will help you determine if and when to participate in the market.

PART FOUR

UNCOMMON ADVICE

14

What Makes Stocks Go Up or Down

When you invest in the market, you should pay attention to anything that may affect your stocks. Some events seem to come out of nowhere—perhaps a terrorist attack, a war, or a recession will cause havoc with the stock market. If there is anything the markets hates, it is uncertainty. One of the reasons the most recent bear market lasted so long was that no one knew when the recession would end, whether we would win the war on terrorism, and whether the United States was going to war. Any one of these events can send the market lower as investors seek protection in cash, gold, or real estate.

As an investor or trader, you must be aware of outside events. Sometimes it helps to step back and see the bigger economic picture. If you can anticipate how an event could affect the stock market, you can shift your money into more profitable investments. Some pros believe that having a thorough understanding of the investment environment is more important than picking the right stock.

The Federal Reserve System: A Government Group You Can't Ignore

The Federal Reserve System (the Fed) is so powerful that anything it does influences the stock market. Often, you will hear more about the actions of the Federal Reserve Board (FRB), a seven-member group that directs the actions of the Federal Reserve System.

The Fed has many duties, including monitoring the economy for problems (especially inflation or deflation) and controlling the country's money supply. It has a powerful tool that directly affects the stock and bond markets—the ability to raise or lower interest rates. The Fed doesn't lower or raise interest rates by flipping a switch. Instead, it either buys or sells millions of dollars worth of Treasury securities, which allows it to adjust interest rates.

Why is this so important? When the Fed lowers interest rates, it means that it will be cheaper for people to borrow money. After all, many Americans love to borrow. When interest rates are lower, more people can afford to buy a house. After they buy their house, they also need furniture, housewares, and appliances. The more money consumers and businesses spend, the better it is for the economy.

Therefore, when interest rates are lowered, the stock market often goes up. Conversely, when interest rates are raised, the stock market tends to go down. Beginning in the 1990s, the Fed began to raise interest rates, a quarter to a half point at a time. The idea was to poke a hole in the "irrationally exuberant" bull market, which was rising faster than anyone had ever imagined. The market seemingly ignored the Fed and continued to go higher.

Finally, in early 2000, the market responded to the multiple interest-rate increases. The Nasdaq began to fall by hundreds, then thousands, of points. The Fed, which had so diligently raised interest rates, frantically began to lower them.

There's an old saying, "Don't fight the Fed," that is known by most investors, but unfortunately this advice didn't work the way it had in the past. Once again, the markets seemingly ignored the actions of the Fed, continuing to plummet. As a result of the lower interest rates, however, the real estate market boomed, and many people took the opportunity to refinance their homes.

If you are watching the stock market, it is always a big deal if the Fed raises or lowers interest rates. The market may rally on news of a rate cut or fall on news of a rise in the rates. Often, the market moves dramatically in advance of a Fed decision.

There is something else you should know about the Fed. Technically, it isn't supposed to care about the stock market, and if you ask the board members, they will say that they are not influenced by the market. But it's an open secret that they do pay attention. If the Fed hadn't intervened with drastic interest rate cuts, the market might have gone down a lot faster and farther than it did. The bottom line is, if you are in the stock market, you should pay attention to what the Fed does.

The Dollar: I'm Falling and I Can't Get Up

One economic indicator that you should keep your eye on is the dollar. When the dollar is strong against other currencies, like the yen and the euro, foreign investors will buy our Treasuries and invest in our stock market. That's the good news. The bad news is that the strong dollar makes our goods undesirable to foreigners because they are so expensive. A strong dollar also makes it hard for people to travel to the United States because it is so expensive.

On the other hand, when the dollar is falling and is weak against other currencies, foreigners pull their money out of our stock market. (Basically, they get hit twice, once when their U.S. stocks fall in price, and again when they lose money on the currency.) As the dollar falls, the stock market tends to go down in price. This is also not a good time to travel overseas, as it will be more expensive. Perhaps the only positive thing that comes from a weak dollar is that foreigners can now afford to buy our goods and services, which pleases American manufacturers.

If you are in the markets, keep your eye on the strength or weakness of the dollar. If you see the dollar falling, as it did in 2002, this is a clue that foreign investors may get spooked and begin pulling their money out of our stock market.

Inflation

Inflation simply refers to how much the prices of the goods and services that you buy go up each year. It is usually written as a percentage. When you study economics, you hear a lot about inflation. One of the reasons that people invest in the stock market is to try to beat inflation.

For example, suppose inflation is currently at 1 percent. That means that it will cost you 1 percent more than the year before to buy goods and services. When you go shopping, you find that groceries, cars, and home appliances have gone up in price from the year before. Because of inflation, the McDonald's hamburger that cost you 10 cents in 1959 now costs you $1.20. A seat at the movies that cost 25 cents back in 1960 now costs $10.00! Now that is inflation!

Too much inflation is not good for the economy, which is why the markets don't like it. It means that people are getting less for their dollars. Conversely, low inflation is good for consumers because they can afford to borrow, charge purchases on credit cards, and buy houses. The more consumers spend, the better it is for the economy.

Economists are generally pleased if inflation remains at no more than 3 or 4 percent, although in 1980 inflation went as high as 18 percent. In addition, the Fed responds by raising interest rates, which restricts the flow of money into the economy. In periods of inflation, the price of investments such as certificates of deposit (CDs) and money market accounts rises (when the Fed raises interest rates to combat inflation, fixed-income investments that are dependent on interest rates move higher).

One of the reasons that investing in the stock market is a good idea is that historically the market has returned 11 percent a year, handily beating inflation. Of course, there is no guarantee that the stock market will come close to returning 11 percent this year or next. On the other hand, if you see inflation rising, that could be a clue for you to move some of your money out of the market and into alternative investments to stocks like a money market account or short-term Treasuries.

Economic Indicators

The government has ways to measure whether the prices of goods and services are rising or falling. For example, the consumer price index (CPI) measures changes in everyday prices like those of food, housing, and clothing. Some people refer to it as the "inflation number" or the "cost-of-living" index. If the CPI goes up, this means that inflation is rising.

The producer price index (PPI) determines whether inflation is rising or falling by measuring the prices of commodities, including raw materials like steel and aluminum. If the prices of raw materials are going up, consumers will ultimately pay more at the supermarket and the gas station.

In addition to the CPI and PPI reports, the U.S. Department of Labor issues the closely watched *unemployment report*. The results of this report directly influence the stock market. If the unemployment rate is low—under 6 percent—there are many jobs available. If the unemployment rate is high—over 6 percent—the job market is tight and it's hard to find jobs. On the day these reports are released, the market reacts in unpredictable ways. In general, the market likes to see low CPI and PPI numbers and a decrease in unemployment.

There are many other reports released by the government that are watched closely by investors and traders. For example, the gross domestic product (GDP) is a quarterly report that measures the quantity of goods and services being produced in our economy. The GDP is a useful but broad barometer of how the economy is doing. The higher the GDP (expressed as a percentage), the faster the economy is growing. If GDP is growing by more than 3 percent, the economy is on the right track. If GDP is negative, either the economy is not growing or we could be in a *recession* (defined as two or more quarters of negative GDP).

Deflation: An Unusual Nightmare

To understand deflation, let's review what we mean by inflation. When the price of goods rises each year, when everything costs more, this is inflation. Deflation, on the other hand, can be defined as an economic condition in which the supply of money and credit is reduced. Although inflation is common, deflation is quite rare in the United States (Japan, however, has been in a deflationary environment for years).

To the uninformed, deflation seems like a good thing. The prices of nearly everything fall as the supply of goods piles up. Manufacturers are forced to cut prices even further to entice shoppers to buy. On the other hand, companies cut employees, real estate prices fall (because borrowers cannot pay back their loans), and the stock market goes through a rough period. Prices are low, but few people have the money to buy anything. Those who do have money tend to wait for prices to drop even further.

For a worst-case scenario of what could happen in a deflationary crash, read Robert Prechter's book *Conquer the Crash* (John Wiley & Sons, 2002). One of the best ways to protect yourself against deflation is to get out of debt. That means paying off your credit cards, your car loans, and your mortgage (although you should talk to a tax adviser before doing the last of these). In addition, force yourself to save more. If we really do have a deflationary crash, those with the most cash will prosper. Because deflation is rare in the United States, there is no need to panic—at least, not yet. Just keep a close eye on economic conditions and be prepared to act if things get dicey.

Politics: The Government Influences the Stock Market

The actions of the president and Congress affect the stock market. Whether it is a major presidential speech, higher taxes, or a new law, how the market reacts depends on how Wall Street interprets the news. After all, the market is based more on perception and psychology than reality. Politics is so intertwined with the financial markets that it would take a political scientist to explain it all.

Other Reasons Stocks
Go Up or Down

The most obvious reason that a stock goes up or down has to do with how much money the corporation makes. If a company is making money or might make money in the future, more people will buy shares of its stock. The name of the game is supply and demand.

Because of supply and demand, when there are more buyers than sellers, the stock price will go up. If there are more sellers than buyers, the stock price will go down. This is Capitalism 101, the heart of our financial system. (Just think of all the books you no longer have to read.) At the end of each market day, many financial experts will try to explain why the market went up or down, but their explanations often have little to do with what really happened.

Often stocks go up or down based primarily on people's perceptions. This is why so many corporations spend a lot of money on advertising and on actions that will bring them positive publicity. This is also why some shareholders send out emails to strangers or post messages in Internet chat rooms to try to convince people to buy more stock.

Stocks also go up or down depending on the mood of the country and the state of the economy. Once again, a lot is based on perception. If people believe that economic conditions are improving and the country is on the right track, they will be more inclined to invest in the stock market. Conversely, the recent bear market has continued because people are wary of the direction of the country, the increased threat of terrorism and war, and a feeling that we were in a recession.

In the next chapter, you will learn where to go (and whom to avoid) for investment advice.

15

Why Investors Lose Money

I've learned a lot from interviewing some of the top traders and investors in the country, as well as from my own mistakes and successes in the stock market. Unfortunately, no matter how many times you try to stop people from losing money in the market, they often don't listen until it's too late. It is only after losing most of their money that they finally admit that they made mistakes.

There is nothing wrong with or unusual about making mistakes. Actually, the biggest mistake you can make is not recognizing that you made one. The most obvious clue that something is going wrong with your investments is that you are losing money. A loss of more than 10 percent on an investment is a signal you have a problem. Remember this: You do not invest in the stock market in order to lose money. The goal of this chapter, therefore, is to help you avoid making the mistakes that trip up and ruin most investors and traders. Most of the time, our worst enemy is ourselves.

Mistake #1: You Don't Sell Your Losing Stocks

For a variety of reasons, some people hold onto their losing stocks too long. Failure to get out of losing positions early is probably the number one reason why so many investing and trading accounts are destroyed. The reasons people hold onto losing stocks are primarily psychological. If you sell a stock for a loss, you deride yourself for not having sold sooner. Adding insult to injury, you have to admit that you lost money. No matter what price you sold the stock at, it always seems as though you could have done better. Many people think they can't be wrong about their stock picks or are seduced by hope and greed. Others convince themselves that a stock will come back one day or are afraid to "throw in the towel."

During the bull market, not only did people *not* get out when their stocks fell 10 or 15 percent, but they bought even more shares. Although there was still plenty of time to get out of the market with minor losses, many people refused to sell their losing stocks. It took 3 years of a bear market before many people realized that they had held on too long. (By the time you've lost 80 or 90 percent of your investment, perhaps it really is too late to sell unless you want a tax write-off.)

To keep your losses small, you need a plan before you buy your first stock. One rule is so important that you should post it in front of your computer or on your desk: If you lose more than 10 percent on an investment, sell. You lost, so you sell the stock. You can put in a stop loss order at 10 percent below the purchase price when you buy the stock, or you can make a mental note. The main point is that you take action when your stock is losing money. (Some stock experts, such as William O'Neil, publisher of *Investor's Business Daily,* recommend selling losing stocks at 8 percent.) Even if the company looks fundamentally strong, if the stock is going down (for reasons that may not be immediately apparent), there is only one response: Use the 10 percent rule.

(There are exceptions, of course. If you buy a stock at what appears to be the bottom and it makes a long sideways move before losing 10 percent, it is acceptable to hold it, especially if you anticipate future gains. The 10 percent rule is designed to prevent undisciplined investors and traders from letting a small loss turn into a large one.)

Mistake #2: You Let Your Winning Stocks Turn into Losers

It seems as if you can't win no matter when you sell. If you sell a stock for a gain, you are left with the lingering feeling that if you had held it a little longer, you'd have made more money. In contrast, some people made tons of money in the stock market, then sat back and watched helplessly while all their profits disappeared (what the market gives, the market takes away). Some are still in denial about the fact that many of their favorite stocks will never return to even. Many people lost not only their gains but their original investment as well. For these people, it would have been less painful to have never made money in the market at all than to have won and lost it all.

Let's take another look at Ericsson, the Swedish telecommunications company. You could have bought the stock for $20 in 1998. From there, Ericsson stock took off, reaching a high of $90 per share a year later. If you were either lucky or a genius, you would have sold all your shares at $90 and gone on vacation. Instead, most people held onto Ericsson as it dropped in price until it traded for less than a dollar a share in 2002 before initiating a 1-for-10 reverse stock split. Thousands of Swedish and American investors lost their shirts on Ericsson (as well as on hundreds of other technology stocks). What did investors do wrong?

If you have a winning stock, you probably think it's crazy to get out too early. That's why you might want to adopt an incremental sell approach. I call it the "30-30" plan: If your stock rises by more than 30 percent, sell 30 percent of your position. By selling a portion of your gains, you satisfy the twin emotions of fear and greed. (Legendary contrarian investor Ted Warren taught that there's never a bad time to take a profit. He summed up this approach when he wrote, "Selling too soon is good insurance against holding a stock too long.")

Do you know how many trillions of dollars would have been saved in the market if people had sold some of their stocks on the way up? Unfortunately, most people do not have the discipline to sell a winning stock at the top. They are afraid of taxes, they don't want to miss out if the stock goes higher, or they get overconfident.

If you make so much money on a stock that you are nearly giddy (called the high-five effect), sell 30 percent of your winnings. By doing so, you lock in at least a portion of your gains, and you can reevaluate your portfolio later. As traders like to say, "You can't go broke taking a profit."

Mistake #3: You Get Too Emotional about Your Stock Picks

Inability to control their emotions is the main reason why most people should not participate in the stock market. When investing in the market with substantial money at stake, many people are flooded with emotions that compel them to make the wrong decisions. In fact, becoming too emotional about your investments is a clue that you could lose money. Making money should be as boring as waiting in line at the supermarket.

A common problem, and one that especially afflicts those who have tasted success in the market, is overconfidence. Although some self-confidence is necessary if you are going to invest in the market, allowing your ego to get in the way of your investing is a dangerous sign. One of the reasons the bull market was destined to end so abruptly was that too many people were making too much money and thought they were geniuses. An old but true saying is, "There are no geniuses in a bull market." The point is that people thought they were geniuses, but in fact they were just being carried by the strength of a bull market.

Before the bull market's abrupt end, many investors got so greedy that they couldn't think straight. They were convinced that the good times would last forever. The signs of greed were everywhere:

- A 15-year-old boy, Jonathon Lebed, made a million dollars pumping and dumping penny stocks. The SEC allowed him to keep half his profits.
- The CEOs of dozens of companies were paid hundreds of millions of dollars in salary and compensation, even though their compa-

nies were losing money. (Many made their millions through stock options, which although legal, did not seem fair to shareholders who lost money.)

- Thousands of people were quitting their jobs to become day traders.
- Stock prices in companies that had no earnings were doubling and tripling each day.
- Many mutual funds were going up by over 100 percent a year.
- Books with titles like *Dow 36,000* and *Dow 100,000* were best-sellers, along with many books on day trading.
- Stock analysts and CEOs were treated like rock stars.
- Car dealers couldn't sell SUVs fast enough, it seemed as though everyone was going to Europe, Starbucks was filled with people starting investment clubs, and people couldn't keep their eyes off financial television programs like CNBC, Bloomberg, and CNNfn.

As the Dow and the Nasdaq plummeted, greed was replaced by hope. In the award-winning movie *The Shawshank Redemption,* the movie character Red (played by Morgan Freeman) said, "Hope is a dangerous thing." In love as in life, there is always hope that things will work out in the end, but in the stock market, hope can destroy your portfolio. If the only reason you are holding onto a stock is because of hope (and not for fundamental or technical reasons), you are going to lose money.

The famous speculator Jesse Livermore once said, "People are hopeful when they should be afraid and are afraid when they should be hopeful." Livermore understood the short-term psychology of the markets about as well as anyone.

The most profitable traders and investors are unemotional about the stocks they buy. They don't rely on fear, greed, or hope when they make trading decisions; they look only at technical and fundamental data. In 1929 and 1987, there was real fear in the stock market. People thought that their stocks were going to zero, and they wanted to get out of the market at any price. Just when people thought that all was lost, 1987 turned out to be the start of a particularly strong market. In 2000, on the other hand, people were much too hopeful when they really should have been afraid.

Mistake #4: You Bet All Your Money on Only One or Two Stocks

One of the problems with investing directly in the stock market is that most people don't have enough money to maintain a properly diversified portfolio. (In general, no one stock should make up more than 10 percent of your portfolio.) Although diversification limits your upside gains, it also protects you in case one of your investments does badly.

If you can't afford to buy more than one or two stocks, you have several choices. First, you can buy mutual funds, especially index funds, which allow you to buy the entire market for a fraction of what it would cost if you bought each stock in the index. Second, you can hire a certified investment adviser to manage your portfolio and help you to diversify.

If you feel that you must bet all your money on only one or two stocks, then buy stocks in conservative companies with low P/Es (less than 10) that pump up their returns with quarterly dividends. You want stocks in companies that are so good that they will be profitable for years.

The Exceptions

If you are a short-term trader (or perhaps a gambler), making big bets on one or two stocks can pay off big. For example, some traders focus on one stock, perhaps an exchange-traded fund (ETF) like QQQQ, Diamonds (DIA), or SPDRs. When you become an expert on only one investment, you have a better idea of when to buy and sell it. Obviously, this strategy is better suited to traders than to investors.

It is also true that if you bet all your money on one stock and you win, you can make a small fortune. However, using this strategy is more akin to gambling than to investing. Although the odds are better than in Las Vegas, it is still risky to bet everything on one investment. To protect yourself, you might be better off betting all your money on a successful mutual fund than on one stock.

Mistake #5: You Are Unable to Be Both Disciplined and Flexible

Almost every professional investor will rightly claim that a lack of discipline is the main reason that most people lose money in the market. If you are disciplined, you have a strategy, a plan, and a set of rules, and no matter what you are feeling, you stick to your strategy, plan, and rules. Discipline means having the knowledge to know what to do (the easy part) and the willpower and courage to actually do it (the hard part). It means that you have to stick to your strategy and obey your rules. This has always worked for successful investors and mutual fund managers.

Although the pros are right in claiming that you need discipline if you are to be successful in the market, you also need to balance this with a healthy dose of flexibility. Some investors were so rigidly disciplined about sticking with their stock strategy that they didn't react when the market and their stocks turned against them. In the name of discipline, many investors went down with the sinking ship. Discipline is essential, but you must be realistic enough to realize that you could be wrong. You have to be flexible enough to change your strategy, your plan, and your rules, especially if you are losing money. For every rule and strategy, there are exceptions. It takes a really exceptional investor to be both disciplined and flexible.

Mistake #6: You Don't Learn from Your Mistakes

Most experienced investors and traders know that you learn more from your losers than from your winners. One of the worst things that happened to many novice investors in the late 1990s was that they made money in the market too quickly and easily. When the easy money stopped and the market plunged, many of them had no idea what to do next. Why? They didn't know how it felt to lose money. Because they had made money the wrong way, they were destined to give it all back. Losing money can be good for you (as long as you don't lose all of it).

It is worth losing a little money in the market today to protect yourself from losing a fortune tomorrow.

If you lose more than 10 percent in the market, there are a few things you can do. Instead of burying your head in the sand, take the time to understand your mistakes. It's not useful to make excuses and act as if your stock losses are only paper losses that will be made up in the future. In the market, everything doesn't always work out in the end. Accept the loss and make sure you don't make the same mistake again.

Next, closely review your investment strategy. You should study the entire market environment and analyze each of the stocks you are holding. If your investments don't hold up based on technical and fundamental analysis, you might want to make changes to your portfolio.

Mistake #7: You Listen to or Get Tips from the Wrong People

If your eyes glaze over when you read about fundamental or technical analysis, there is a simpler way to find stocks to buy—stock tips. The beauty of tips is that you can make money without doing any work. If this sounds too good to be true, it is.

In fact, one of the easiest ways to lose money in the market is by listening to tips, especially if they come from well-meaning but uninformed relatives or acquaintances. These people often become cheerleaders for a stock, trying to convince you to buy it. Because it's hard to say no to easy money (especially when the tip comes from a trusted source), there are some steps you can take to limit your risks.

First, you should never act on a tip before doing fundamental or technical research. One look at a stock chart should give you a good idea as to whether the stock is a loser. As I reported before, most people spend more time researching a new television than a stock. Many people wouldn't think twice about spending $20,000 on a stock tip but will spend a month researching a $200 television set. If you do receive a "can't lose" tip that is impossible to resist, buy in small quantities— no more than 100 shares. If the tip turns out to be a dud (and it probably will), you've lost only a little money, and you've also learned a valuable lesson.

Should you get your stock picks from experts? Don't forget that most of the experts who appeared on television or were quoted in magazines were terrible stock pickers. Analysts lied, economists misjudged the economy, CEOs were overly optimistic, and accounting firms fudged the numbers to make losing companies look like winners.

At the same time, greedy and lazy investors (and we're almost all guilty) must take responsibility for buying stocks based on tips. ("Everyone wanted to be a player but we ended up being played.") The best advice I ever received on the market was also the simplest: Keep your ears shut.

Mistake #8: You Follow the Crowd

Do you want to lose money? Then do what everyone else is doing. Unfortunately, it is excruciatingly difficult to think differently from everyone else. If you study the lives of some of the greatest traders and investors in the recent past, you will find that they often made their fortunes by doing the opposite of what the crowd was doing. That means buying when other people are selling and selling when other people are buying.

If you study the psychology of group behavior, you find many periods and events in history that attest to herd mentality—or the "madness of crowds," as one author put it. Although the crowds *can* win, they don't win for long. As mentioned earlier, the signal that a bull market is ending is that it seems as though everyone is in the market. Conversely, a signal of a bear market's end is that people are too afraid to invest in the market. When almost everyone is avoiding the stock market, and it seems like perhaps the worst possible time to invest, the bear market will end. Unfortunately, no one rings a bell to announce the end. You have to figure it out for yourself.

So how do you think differently from the crowd? You can start by taking a look at strategies that most people don't use. For example, you could buy covered call options on stocks you own, trade ETFs, or short stocks. Although these strategies are not recommended for average investors, those of you who have the time to do additional research may find that taking a different approach can be profitable. Unfortunately, once everyone finds out about them, many strategies cease to work. (For example, strategies like the "January effect," where you sell your stocks in early December and buy them back in January, worked for years—that is, until it was widely reported in the media.)

Keep in mind that perceptions about the market change very rapidly. From a state of near euphoria about the market, the crowd has become ornery and pessimistic. A few clues: The public's interest in books about the stock market has declined; many people no longer want to talk about the market except to tell you how much money they lost; and many people are showing the effects of a reverse wealth effect, as seen in a decline in the sales of boats, SUVs, and other luxury items. If you are a contrarian, when the public has thrown in the towel, you'll begin to look for buying opportunities.

Mistake #9: You Aren't Prepared for the Worst

Before you get into the market, you should be prepared, not scared. Although you should always hope for the best, you must be prepared for the worst. The biggest mistake many investors make is thinking that their stocks won't go down. They are not prepared for an extended bear market, a recession, deflation, a market crash, or an unanticipated event that will ruin the market. Even if you don't expect a financial disaster, create a "crash-proof" plan based on logic and common sense, not fear. Here are a few steps you can take to protect your portfolio:

1. *Move more of your money into cash.* When you are in cash (including Treasury bills if the economy gets really terrifying), it's easy to make unemotional decisions about where to put your money next. Cash is a comfortable place to be when the economy is struggling and the market is falling. Temporarily waiting on the sidelines in cash until the market recovers can be a wise move. If the market really does capitulate (or we get locked into a deflationary nightmare), one way to win is to be flush with cash when stocks are selling at bargain-basement prices.

2. *Trade less.* If you are a trader, you should limit the number of shares that you trade. As it becomes more difficult to make money in the market, some people mistakenly try to win back their lost profits. Greed is more powerful than fear, which is why some people will mortgage the house for a chance to get rich quickly. If you must trade, trade with less.
3. *Study more.* If we do enter into a lengthy bear market, use the time to study the markets, read books, and brush up on fundamental and technical analysis. When the market does come back (it always does eventually), you'll be prepared with a handful of new stock picks.

Mistake #10: You Miss Out or Mismanage Money

Managing money is a difficult skill for most people, but it's one of the most important skills to have. Unfortunately, if you can't manage money, you're destined to have financial problems (unless you hire someone to manage it for you). In the end, it's not how much you make but how much you *keep* that matters. Do you want to know the secret to making money in the stock market or with any investment? *Don't lose money.* (Don't laugh—it's true.) If you think about it long enough, you'll realize that this makes a lot of sense. Obviously, it's not easy to find investments where you don't lose money, but that shouldn't stop you from trying.

Just as harmful as mismanaging money is missing out on money-making opportunities. A little bit of fear keeps you on your toes, but too much fear can cause you to miss out on profitable investments or trades. It's the fear of loss that prevents many people from buying at the bottom. It's the fear of missing out on higher profits that prevents people from selling before it's too late. Usually, fear results from a lack of information. That is why it's essential that you do your own research when a financial opportunity comes your way. This gives you an opportunity to make an informed decision based on the facts, not on emotion.

Obviously, you aren't privy to all the information that you need in order to be 100 percent right. You have to make a decision based on the best information you have at the time. Many times you'll be wrong.

One of my friends calls it the "Swiss cheese principle." Often, you don't have enough information to make a completely risk-free decision, but you still must act. There are so many holes—or missing pieces of information—that you can only wonder if you are making the right decision. The fear of losing prevents some people from making any decision at all. And yet, you still must act.

The Dutch Tulip Bulb Mania*

A *bubble* is a phenomenon in which investors and traders buy stocks or other items at such a feverish pace that the market rises to irrational levels. The buyers seem to be under a mass delusion that the market will only go higher. Before long, speculators hoping for quick profits jump in, creating a mania. Eventually, investors come back to their senses, causing a selling panic. There have been a handful of bubbles in history, all of which have ended quite badly for investors.

One of the most spectacular bubbles in history occurred in Holland in the seventeenth century. In 1635 people were suddenly willing to pay any amount in order to own a single tulip bulb. These bulbs had become status symbols for the rich and famous. Some bulbs were beautiful mutations, what the Dutch called "bizarres" (*Famous Financial Fiascos,* by John Train). Speculators would buy one, then immediately sell it for a higher price.

As the tulip mania increased, speculators pushed the prices higher. For example, to buy one exotic tulip bulb, you would have to exchange several horses, pigs, bread, a carriage, tons of cheese, beer, and house furnishings (using today's exchange rate, well over $200,000). Many investors were more than willing to trade their houses or valuable paintings for one tulip bulb. There was always a bigger fool willing to pay a higher price for the bulb. The entire country got swept up in the mania.

---

*Some of the text used in this sidebar originally appeared in my first book, *101 Investment Lessons by the Wizards of Wall Street* (Career Press, 1999).

As with most bubbles, most people didn't know they're in one until it was too late. At the time, people thought the tulips were wise investments that would last forever. In one sense, the craving for tulip bulbs nearly lasted forever. Today, the Dutch export millions of dollars worth of tulip bulbs to other countries—but at more reasonable prices.

This bubble popped rather abruptly and dramatically. People stopped and looked around and wondered how anyone could pay that much for an exotic flower. It was similar to a game of musical chairs when the music stops. People who only a few months before hadn't been able to buy the tulip bulbs fast enough now couldn't sell them in time. Family fortunes were wiped out, there was widespread panic, and the Dutch economy collapsed.

The closest the U.S. stock market came to a bubble occurred during the Internet mania. It seemed as if the entire country was deluded into thinking that every Internet stock would go up. Companies like Excite at Home, Pets.com, HomeGrocer.com, and hundreds of others were bid up to ridiculously high valuations. At the time, some Internet companies with no earnings had a higher market cap than some of the largest corporations in America.

Just like the tulip bubble, the Internet bubble ended abruptly. Investors also looked around and wondered how they could have paid so much for companies with little or no earnings. Some people are still holding shares of Internet companies that may never come back to even.

In the next chapter, you will learn my thoughts about the stock market.

16

What I Really Think about the Stock Market

Because I'm not on anyone's permanent payroll, I am free to tell you what I really think about the stock market. You don't have to agree with what I say—in fact, I welcome opposing viewpoints. There is no one right answer when it comes to the stock market. In the end, you should make up your own mind where to invest your money.

Listen to Traders, Not Investors

If you want to hear the truth (no matter how painful it is), listen to short-term traders who are in cash by the end of the week. Because traders don't care whether the market goes up or down, they are usually more objective about the direction of the market.

In contrast, most long-term investors are perpetually hopeful that next year or in 5 years the market will be higher. This includes anyone who works on Wall Street or is heavily invested in the market. These people will almost always tell you that the markets are going nowhere but up. For the sake of their portfolios, I hope they are right, but hope never made anyone a dime in the market. (To be fair, however, I have also listened to my share of blowhard day traders, who think they are geniuses right before they destroy their account.)

Keep a Lot of Cash

In an irrational world, holding cash makes you think rationally, especially if we're headed toward a recession or a bear market. Even in a bull market, keep a little cash on the side. When you hold cash, you know that you can pay your bills and take care of any unexpected emergencies. In addition, in the event of a crash or economic crisis, your cash will allow you to invest at bargain prices.

When you have diversified into cash, you aren't affected by the daily gyrations of the market. Also, when the market is ornery and you're unsure of what to do, cash is the best place to be until you make up your mind what to invest in. In my opinion, even a 4 percent annual return is better than losing money. As I said in a previous chapter, making money should be boring. Holding cash is about as boring as it gets.

Psychology Makes the Market Go Round

I'm convinced that the emotions of other investors and traders determine where the market is headed. Most investors and traders agree that in the short term, investor psychology has a dramatic effect on the market. That is why technical analysis, which measures market sentiment, tends to work over short periods.

At the height of the last bull market, the overall perception was that the good times would last forever, even to the point where bad news was spun on Wall Street as being positive. For example, although many Internet companies consistently reported negative earnings, people bid their prices up higher in the anticipation and hope that future earnings would improve. People continued to buy in the hope that many companies (especially Internet and telecommunications companies) would see substantial profits.

As you can guess, for the first 3 years of the subsequent bear market, the reverse occurred. People stopped paying attention to the market to the point where they refused to look at their account statements. Even when a company released positive earnings, the stocks often dropped in price or remained unchanged. In general, people refused to participate in the market.

You need to understand the importance of psychology in the market in order to look for clues that will lead you to profitable investment opportunities as well as to take steps to protect yourself from losing money. This means being aware of what is happening in your city, the country, and the world.

The next bull market will begin when investors are so disgusted and afraid of the market that they've lost all hope that it will ever recover. There will be numerous signs that the market is rallying, but only a handful of people will be savvy enough to connect the dots.

Don't Trust Earnings Estimates

I can't tell you what a company will earn in the next quarter, let alone the next year. There is no way you can tell me that a company is going to be profitable in 5 or 10 years. It amazes me that people act as if they know for a fact how much a company is going to earn in the future. In the past, we depended on accounting firms to certify that the numbers coming from companies were truthful. Once we discovered that there was a conflict of interest between the accounting firms and the audited companies, we couldn't believe anyone's numbers. We're hoping that Wall Street, the accounting firms, and CEOs will give us numbers that we can trust in the future. Until then, let the buyer beware. (It takes extraordinary intuition and information to find out what is really going on behind the scenes at many companies.)

Use Both Technical and Fundamental Analysis

Nearly every book written on the stock market assumes that you will choose between technical and fundamental analysis when deciding what stocks to buy. Guess what? You can use both methods. If you are an investor, you can learn a lot by looking at a stock chart, using technical indicators, and looking at stock patterns. At the same time, you should not buy a stock unless you are convinced that the company's fundamentals are strong. No matter which method you use, you don't want to overpay for the stock.

By using both fundamental and technical analysis, you can study both the company and its stock price. Although there are advantages and disadvantages of using either method, in the end, you have to decide which works best for you. By learning both technical and fundamental analysis, not only will you become a more knowledgeable investor or trader, but you will also have more tools in your toolbox. This could give you an edge over other market participants. Rather than choosing one method or the other, be eclectic.

Losing (a Little) Money Can Be Educational

One of the worst things that happened to many people during the last bull market was that they got the idea that it was easy to beat the market. Before they had a chance to cash in their winnings, most of their profits had disappeared. If you lose money in the stock market (or in any other financial endeavor), turn this event into an educational experience. Losing money has a number of benefits:

1. *It forces you to analyze what you did wrong.* Determine whether the strategies you (or your financial adviser) are using are on the right track.
2. *It tests your character.* If you crunch keyboards or throw things around when you lose money, you had better change investment strategies. Successful investing and trading is not supposed to be exciting—the pros take their gains and losses in stride.
3. *It forces you to be disciplined.* Everyone always talks about the importance of discipline, and there's nothing like losing money to make you realize that you lack it. You failed to limit your losses or protect your winnings.

4. *It forces you to take action.* When you lose money in the market, you have a choice: You can keep repeating the same mistakes, or you can find out what you're doing wrong. You learn nothing if you ignore the truth. If you find out what you're doing wrong, you always have a chance to get it right the next time.

Get Your Finances in Order

In my opinion, you shouldn't consider investing in the market until you've taken care of some other important details. Here are a few ideas:

1. If you can afford it, the first investment you should make is in your home.
2. Next, buy a mutual fund. This will give you a taste of how the stock market operates. If you have a chance to open up a 401(k) or an IRA, do so. Earning tax-free money can eventually make you wealthy.
3. If you have any money left over, invest a portion in the stock market.
4. Your lifelong goal should be to reduce or eliminate debt. It's amazing how quickly your money grows when you are not tied down with unwanted debt, like credit card bills and car payments. (I don't even like mortgage payments, but you had better speak to a tax adviser before making that move.)

Buying and Holding Isn't for Everyone

In my opinion, you should not simply buy a stock and hold it indefinitely. For over 60 years, investors have been brainwashed into using this simple but ineffective strategy. Let's try to understand why buy and hold is so popular.

First, there has been a massive public relations campaign by Wall Street to lure people into buying and holding stocks. If the market is going up, you buy because you could miss out on the next bull market. If the market is going down, you buy because stock prices are so cheap.

When the public invests in the market, it keeps people on Wall Street employed. That is why so few pros advise you not to buy stocks. And if you're not buying, hardly anyone will advise you to sell. Sell a stock? Are you kidding? It will always come back one day, they say. Even now, people are buying and hoping that their portfolios will miraculously come back to even by the time they retire. Many of them will be in for a huge shock.

In the 1990s, it seemed so easy to pick winning stocks. Many advocates of buy and hold point to the successful record of billionaire investor Warren Buffett. What the experts fail to tell you is that Buffett almost never buys the stocks of technology companies, has the skill to take apart and analyze a balance sheet and the patience to stick it out for the long haul, and is willing to wait indefinitely until he gets the price he wants. Unfortunately, it's not easy for people to emulate Buffett. They don't take the time to do the necessary research, they get too emotional about their stock picks, and they get lured into buying the wrong stocks. They'd be better off in a mutual fund that beats both bear and bull markets.

The Market Doesn't Always Go Up

Nearly everyone connected to Wall Street says that the average yearly return on the stock market for the last 60 years is 11 percent (one of the reasons why you should buy and hold forever). The one fact they forget to tell you is that the stocks in nearly all the stock indexes are routinely shifted to make room for more profitable companies. The indexes remove companies that have gone bankrupt, no longer meet the index requirements, or no longer reflect the index's philosophy. In fact, most major indexes make dozens of changes to their listings each year.

If you want to get really picky, of the original Dow 12 stocks in 1896, only General Electric remains in the index. The other companies, such as American Tobacco and U.S. Leather, either went out of business or merged with other companies. I guess you could say that it's anyone's guess how much the market has really gone up or down in the last 100 years. As many people have learned the hard way, buy and hold fails miserably in a bear market. In addition, even if the market goes up, that doesn't mean that *your* stocks will.

The Markets Are Not Fair to Individual Investors

If you are going to participate in the stock market, you have to know the truth: The markets are not fair to individual investors. To learn what really happens on Wall Street, read former SEC Chairman Arthur Levitt's book *Take on the Street: What Wall Street and Corporate America Don't Want You to Know* (Pantheon Books, 2002). It is an inside look at what happens behind the scenes on Wall Street, including political maneuvering, manipulation, lies, distortions, and other schemes designed to keep individual investors in the dark. Many of the worst offenders are company insiders and Wall Street players, including stock analysts, who have access to information that they aren't willing to share with individual investors. The insiders know how to maneuver around the rules.

Martin Weiss, author of *The Ultimate Safe Money Guide* (John Wiley & Sons, 2002), mentions a number of outright fraudulent activities that some companies engage in: padded sales reports, misreported options, fake analyst ratings, and stockbrokers who attempt to swindle clients.

In my opinion, the biggest game of all is trying to convince people that the markets are fair and equitable and that everyone has an equal chance to make money. Some people who are connected to the financial markets attempt to manipulate the markets by passing out false email messages, posting fake messages in Internet chat rooms, calling gullible strangers on the phone, and going on television to pump up a stock.

Others, such as institutional investors or professional traders, will buy or sell huge numbers of shares in a single day just to fool the public into thinking that there is a "rally" or a "correction" in the stock. When the public reacts accordingly, these investors do the opposite.

Of course it doesn't have to be this way. It will take a combination of government intervention (including a stronger and well-financed Securities and Exchange Commission), politicians who are willing to stand up to Wall Street's special interests, and investors who are unwilling to participate in a rigged game. Until the market is truly fair, individual investors would be advised to be careful. It will take a long time before many people will trust the markets again. (Perhaps Wall Street likes it that way. If the markets are too dangerous for individual investors, you have no choice but to give your money to the professionals.)

Not Everyone Should Invest in Individual Stocks

Although I believe that people should learn everything they can about the market (which is why I wrote this book), overall I think that most people should be cautious about buying or selling individual stocks. I know this is an unusual conclusion after writing a book about stocks. (And believe me, I know this is not a popular position to take!) In my opinion, there are many less risky things to do with your money than investing it directly in the stock market. It's an extremely tough game to master, and only a few actually succeed at it.

I think that many individual investors don't have the time, the knowledge, or the discipline to buy individual stocks. You can't just buy a stock and go to sleep. You have to closely monitor individual stocks, and, unfortunately, most people don't have the opportunity to do that.

There are many hidden pitfalls that make investing in the stock market risky. Until the markets are truly fair for the individual investor, which isn't likely to happen anytime soon, my advice is to be very wary about investing directly in the market. (This will change when the stock market environment is as fair for individual investors as it is for large investors.)

That doesn't mean, however, that you shouldn't be paying attention to the market. The time will come when out of all the chaos a fair, trustworthy, and investor-friendly market will be created. When the time is right, you might consider investing in individual stocks. Until then, learn everything you can about the market, but don't participate until you fully understand the risks and rewards.

And Yet There Are Exceptions

On the other hand, I don't want to discourage those who feel that they can win the stock market game. If you are excited by the stock market and feel that you can make money at it, by all means, set aside a small amount of money and give it your best shot. You don't need a fortune to make a fortune in the market. (I know a trader who turned $5000 into $500,000 during the bull market.) Even if you make only a couple of hundred dollars a week in the market, the lessons you'll learn will be priceless. As long as you are aware of the risks (that you could lose all your money), go ahead and take a chance. Although most people should be cautious about buying individual stocks, mutual funds makes sense for many people. You can buy mutual funds that go long or short, invest in gold, real estate, or technology, to name a few. An even better idea for many people is Exchange Traded Funds (ETF's).

A Controversial Trading Strategy That Works

Now that we nearly at the end of the book, I'm going to do something different. I'm going to reveal a sophisticated stock trading strategy that works in both bull and bear markets. It's likely that you'll never use the strategy, and you certainly won't use it at first, but understanding how it works may give you an inside look at how some traders attempt to beat the market.

The trading strategy I'm about to reveal is so simple that it will amaze you, although you must be aware that it's controversial. There are a lot of professionals on Wall Street, including many money managers, who have done everything in their power to prevent people from using it. It goes against everything that Wall Street has been preaching for 200 years.

This strategy was discovered by an acquaintance of mine who worked at a midsized company. I was surprised to see his portfolios double and triple, easily beating the returns of nearly every mutual fund. His biggest mistake: A few years ago, he taught the successful strategy to other employees. Before long, half the employees in the company were using the system, disrupting work and annoying those who didn't participate (there's nothing more frustrating than watching coworkers make more money than you). Eventually, the company he worked for refused to let him use the strategy.

Finally, this strategy is not for beginners. To use it, you must monitor the U.S. and international markets closely and make last-minute decisions that could cost you a lot of money if you're wrong.

How the Strategy Works

The strategy is simple: When the U.S. markets are up a lot (approximately 1 percent or more), you move your money from a mutual fund money market account into an international fund. More often than not, the foreign markets (primarily Europe and Asia) will follow the U.S. markets. It is estimated that foreign markets follow the U.S. markets about two-thirds of the time or more.

The strategy works because of the way mutual fund companies price their funds. Instead of updating the net asset value (NAV) of a particular fund the next day, mutual fund companies price their funds on the basis of the previous day's close, called "stale" pricing. The strategy works because of the time difference between U.S. and foreign markets—what some might call a loophole. The 6-hour difference between U.S. and European markets allow you to *arbitrage* the funds (take advantage of the inefficiencies in their prices). According to critic Jason Zweig of *Money* magazine, "It's like knowing tomorrow's news today."

The strategy is known by a variety of names, including time-zone trading, market timing, and in-and-out trading. Gary Smith, author of *How I Trade for a Living* (John Wiley & Sons, 1999), briefly wrote about similar fund trading strategies. However, very few people are aware that the strategy works most efficiently in a 401(k) or 403(b). Although mutual fund companies have been aggressive about stopping people from trading mutual funds in taxable accounts, many have allowed 401(k) and 403(b) plan participants to continue to use this strategy. To my knowledge, no one has ever revealed this secret.

The Rules

1. You begin with a company-sponsored 401(k) or 403(b) tax-deferred savings plan. The beauty of using the strategy in such a plan is that your gains are tax-free. (Although this strategy also works using a regular taxable account, most mutual fund companies penalize you for using market-timing tactics.)

2. Check to make sure that the company you work for allows you to make unlimited and penalty-free exchanges between investment funds.
3. Move all of your cash into a money market account and wait.
4. When the Dow is having a particularly strong day (and it's hoped that the Nasdaq is, too), especially into the close, transfer all or part of your money into a European/Asian mutual fund before 4:00 p.m. Eastern time.
5. Perhaps seven times out of ten, the next day, European markets and sometimes Asian markets will follow the Dow. On a great day, you'll get a 2 percent return (not bad for one day). On a typical day, you'll get 0.5 to 1 percent.
6. If the Dow is still strong for a second day, keep your money in the European fund for another day. Otherwise, transfer all your money back to the money market fund. During a bull market, keeping your money in European/Asian mutual funds for several days was not uncommon. In a bear market, you almost always had to move your money out the next day.
7. When using this system, the most important part of the day is the last 15 minutes of the U.S. market. This is when you decide whether to transfer your money. When you're not sure, you don't move, or you move only 50 percent.
8. Although using this method is sometimes boring, making even 1 percent a week adds up to 52 percent a year. In a bear market, you are lucky to get 0.5 percent a week.
9. The beauty of the system is that you are in cash most of the time and enter the market only when you are confident that the market is going up. Hopefully, you are in cash on the worst market days and are participating in international markets on the best days.

When you use this system, you spend no more than 15 minutes a day deciding whether to enter the market. In a bear market, you are out of the market most of the time. In a bull market, you are in most of the time. It can't get much simpler than that! If you can make as little as 1 or 2 percent a month in the market, a seemingly easy feat, the numbers really add up. (Most pros will tell you that you should buy and hold mutual funds so that you don't miss out on the best days. Although this makes sense, you also want to avoid the worst days!)

You will have to experiment to determine what are the best days to move. For example, some people who use this method don't move on Fridays. Others move only when the Dow is up a huge amount, at least 1.5 percent. Others move if the Dow is up at least 1 percent. You also have to check European markets for any news that could affect the next day's stock prices. Finally, you need to carefully study which countries your European fund is investing in.

What the Critics Say

Mutual fund companies don't like market timers and will do everything in their power to discourage timing strategies. Many of them penalize traders with taxable accounts by tacking on 1 percent penalties if they notice market-timing tactics. [It's also possible that in the future mutual fund companies will tack on penalties if you use this strategy in your 401(k) or 403(b).]

Critics contend that this strategy punishes long-term investors in foreign mutual funds. Jason Zweig wrote in *Money* magazine that in just a few years, short-term mutual fund traders have transferred millions of dollars ($420 million, according to him) from the accounts of long-term investors to their own accounts. Zweig suggests that the strategy, although legal, is unethical and should be stopped. Basically, mutual fund traders are taking advantage of a loophole in the way mutual funds are priced. Others might argue this is simply the capitalist system at work. In the end, you have to judge for yourself whether it is capitalism at work or unethical greed.

As you know from reading this book, mutual funds are supposed to be long-term investments, not vehicles for short-term trading. That is why market timing drives mutual fund managers crazy. They hate it when you transfer money into and out of international funds. Therefore, once they identify you as a market timer, it is likely that you will no longer be allowed to use the strategy.

Although this strategy worked in the past, there is no guarantee that it will work in the future. Just like other market timing strategies that have worked before (e.g., the January effect), once too many people find out about them, they cease to work. In addition, Zweig says that people don't realize how easy it is to lose money when you use this strategy. (On the other hand, when you are wrong, your risks are minimized because you are trading mutual funds, not individual stocks.) Even on the worst days, you probably won't lose more than .5 or 1 percent. Eventually, you will learn the best days to "jump," assuming you are allowed by your 401(k) or 403(b) plan provider. Nevertheless, most experts claim that market-timing strategies do not work.

Why have I spent so much time telling you about a strategy that might not work anymore? First, many mutual fund companies do allow 401(k) and 403(b) plan participants to use this strategy. If you thoroughly understand the risks, rewards, and limitations of using this strategy and don't feel it is unethical, you might want to investigate it further. Second, to be a successful investor or trader, you have to think differently from everyone else. I'm hoping that revealing this strategy will help get you started. (You can also trade ETF's, or invest in funds that do allow timing, such as the Rydex Funds, Pro Funds, or Potomac.)

The Games Analysts Play

There are a few stock analysts we will never forget. This includes analyst Walter Piecyk, with his $1000 a share price target for Qualcomm in 1999 (or $250 if you adjust for a 4-to-1 split). Although he did lower his price target to $200 in 2000, it was too little and too late. The press also had a field day with Henry Blodget, the former Wall Street analyst who put outrageously high price targets on Amazon.com (AMZN) when it was trading at $250 a share. (Ironically, Blodget's price target on Amazon was initially correct. Amazon rose to a split-adjusted high of $678 a share before falling to less than $10 a share.) It wasn't just Blodget who gave Amazon a buy or strong buy rating—30 other analysts made the same call.

Years later, it was reported that while Blodget was publicly telling people to buy many of these overvalued stocks, he was privately writing emails to his colleagues urging them to sell.

"What a POS," he reportedly wrote in one email. Most of the stocks Blodget touted went to under $5 within a year of his recommendation. Meanwhile, his firm paid him more than $12 million for his analysis, perhaps not because of his stock picks but because of the investment banking clients he brought in.

One of the most infamous Internet bulls was stock analyst Mary Meeker. She told anyone who would listen to buy Priceline (PCLN) in 1999, when the stock was trading at $165 a share. She repeated her buy recommendation at $78, and she continuously and publicly told investors to buy until Priceline fell to less than $3 a share. Forget about P/Es, Meeker said. It was reported that Meeker and the Wall Street firm she worked for made millions in fees that year. (Finally, when Priceline was at $3 a share, Meeker told investors to hold.)

Here's how the game was played: The investment banking divisions of the major brokerage firms are paid to raise money for companies, so they strongly encourage the firms' analysts to be bullish on the companies the firms represent. That is why analysts will rarely say anything controversial or negative about a current or future client.

In a scathing report on how analysts do business, the CBS program *60 Minutes* interviewed Tom Brown, an analyst who had been fired by a major Wall Street firm. Brown revealed some of the secrets behind analysts' recommendations. "I don't know frankly how some of these analysts live with themselves," he said at the time. Brown said that it was hard to look at himself in the mirror, knowing that he might have caused some people to lose 50 percent of their retirement money. "They really are cheerleaders," Brown said of analysts. "The investment banking group wants you to be wildly bullish about everybody."

Of course, there were reputable analysts who told investors the truth about the highly inflated technology stocks, especially the Internet stocks. For example, Ashok Kumar, a semiconductor analyst for a Wall Street firm, downgraded Intel from a strong buy to a buy. The stock lost 20 points over a 2-week period. (In the wacky world of Wall Street, a downgrade from strong buy to buy is like issuing a sell recommendation.) Other analysts criticized Kumar's rating and considered the price drop to be a buying opportunity. They were wrong.

Another reputable stock analyst, Dan Niles, turned negative on the telecommunication stocks he was covering. As it turned out, even the public didn't want to listen. It was reported that he received hate mail and threats as he candidly analyzed the telecom sector. On the other hand, dozens more analysts took advantage of investors' greed by making outrageous price calls based on nothing more than pie-in-the-sky stories and ridiculous valuations. If you looked at the fundamentals of many of these companies, it was quite clear that they weren't going to be making money anytime soon, if ever.

Although it is too late for those who got talked into buying many of the Internet stocks at the top, there are many lessons to be learned from the games analysts play. If you are going to invest in the stock market, it is essential that you understand how upgrades and downgrades influence a stock, and that you learn about the incestuous relationship that analysts have with the investment banking divisions of the brokerage companies.

The SEC has talked about eliminating the conflict of interest that exists between investment bankers and the analysts in the research department. Until the system is changed, however, you can't trust what analysts or their research departments say about stocks.

Conclusion

Before you attempt to buy your first stock, be aware that you are entering a battlefield populated by sharks that want your money. If you are going to invest in the market, you must fight them with knowledge (a very effective shark repellant). If you aren't willing to do your own homework (independently do research on companies and stocks) and must depend on a stockbroker or a stranger on television to tell you what stocks to buy or sell, you are destined to lose money. You have no one to blame but yourself when you do.

If you lose money, the government won't help you, nor will anyone on Wall Street. Remember that making money in the stock market is serious business. It is as serious as raising children or working at a full-time job. In the end, you must take responsibility for your own investments. You're completely on your own.

In the past, many investors and traders made money in the market but had no clue as to how they were doing it. "I'm doing nothing, and look how much money I'm making," several investors told me. You should not be surprised to learn that many of these people lost everything. In a few years, people will be lulled into thinking that it's safe to participate in the market again. The historic $8 trillion in losses will be forgotten. My hope is that after you read this book, you won't make the same mistakes that millions of other people made in the past.

Now that you are aware of the risks as well as the rewards, you have a choice. If you are willing to take the time to learn what works on Wall Street, you can survive and prosper as a twenty-first-century investor. To win, you have to be faster, more knowledgeable, and more flexible than investors in the past. As soon as you put down this book, begin thinking and planning. Don't stop until you have created a successful portfolio. My advice is to keep it simple.

On the other hand, if you decide that stocks are not for you, at least you have a better understanding of how the stock market works. This is information that should help you no matter what you decide to do in the future. Always be on the lookout for profitable money-making opportunities while remaining cautious. When in doubt, however, don't do it.

Finally, I have learned from experience that the best investment you can make is in people. You can't go wrong spending money on a college education, your home, a new business, your children, or those who desperately need your help. After all, why make money if you don't use it to improve your life or the lives of others?

It's been a pleasure sharing my knowledge with you. I wish all of you the best of luck and hope that all your financial dreams come true.

Knowledge: The Greatest Gift You Can Give Your Loved Ones

After my father passed away last year, I found a letter written by my grandfather, Charles Sincere, the successful owner of a Chicago stock brokerage firm. The letter, with the title "Open on Your 21st Birthday," contained the following financial advice (my grandfather also referred to a *Wall Street Journal* article in his letter to my father).

1. Begin by paying off all your debts.
2. After being debt-free, you must not be tempted to blow your money on risky financial ventures.
3. It is hard enough for most people to earn a bare living, including 95 percent who are unable to keep and acquire a fortune. This is not to discourage you but to warn you and give you courage to fight harder to be one of the 5 percent.
4. Always be prepared for the possibility that you may have to support your parents. In addition, you owe it to your wife and family to buy life insurance.
5. You want the privilege of helping those who are afflicted and impoverished.
6. The most important measure of success is integrity, hard work, and being right more than 55 percent of the time. This also means diversifying risks so that when you are wrong it won't break or crimp you.
7. Never cosign promissory notes to help others.
8. Never buy stocks in small corporations to please friends— easy to buy, hard to sell.
9. Don't be easy in loaning money except in extreme cases (i.e., don't let a worthy friend down).
10. Only hard experience, proven by facts, should impress you and cause you to follow the rules just outlined.

Index

AAA bonds, 20–21
Advice, 164–165, 171, 187
After-hours trading, 53
Amazon.com, 183
American Stock Exchange (AMEX), 6, 7, 84
Annual reports, 93, 95–96
Arbitrage, 180
Ask price, 51–52
Asset allocation, 38–39
Assets, 93, 94
Averaging down, 72

Balance sheets, 93–94
Bar charts, 110–111
Bear markets, 27
Bearish patterns, 120–123
Berkshire Hathaway, 40–41, 104
Bid price, 51–52
Bills, 20
Blodget, Henry, 183–184
Bogle, John, 40
Boiler Room (film), 34
Boiler rooms, 33–34
Bollinger bands, 137–138
Bond rating, 21
Bonds, 19–21, 20

Boston Stock Exchange, 7
Bottom fishing, 71–72
Breakaway gap, 126
Brokerage firms:
    discount, 57–58
    full-service, 55–57
    going on margin with, 63–64
    investment banking divisions of, 184
    opening account with, 58
    and order types, 58–61
    placing orders with, 61–62
Brown, Tom, 184
Bubbles, 168–169
"Bucket shops," 128
Buffett, Warren, 8–9, 52, 70, 89, 95, 104–105, 176
Bull markets, 27–28
Bullish patterns, 121–124
Buttonwood Agreement, 6
Buy-and-hold strategy, 70–71, 175–176
Buy-on-the dip strategy, 71

Call options, 81–82
Candlestick charts, 111, 112
CANSLIM, 75–76
Capital gains, 5
Capital loss, 5

Capitulation, 144–145
Cash, 25–26, 166, 172
Certificates of deposit (CDs), 25, 152
*Characteristics and Risks of Standard-
    ized Options,* 83
Charts:
    bar, 110–111
    candlestick, 111, 112
    line, 109–110
    stock, 108–109
Chicago Board Options Exchange
    Volatility Index (VIX), 142–143
Chicago Mercantile Exchange (the
    Merc), 139
Churchill, Winston, 107
Churchill (James C. Humes), 107
Churning, 56
Cincinnati Stock Exchange, 7
Commercial paper, 25
Commission-based system, 56
Commissions, 6, 56
Commodities, 138–139
Common stocks, 5
Compound earnings, 39
Compounding, 39–40
Conquer the Crash (Robert Prechter),
    154
Consolidating stock, 114
Consumer price index (CPI), 153
Continuation gap, 126
Contrarian investing, 74, 142–144
Coolidge administration, 65
Corporate bonds, 20
Corporate insiders, 92–93
Corporations, 5, 8
Cost, stock, 13
Coupons, 20
Covered calls, writing, 83–84
Covering your position, 79
CPI (consumer price index), 153
Crash(es), market:
    of 1929, 65–66, 144, 161
    of 1987, 57, 144, 161
Crowd, following the, 165–166

Day traders/trading, 9, 57, 77–78
Debt, 154
Decimalization, 52
Deflation, 153–154
Detailed stock quotes, 50–52
DIA (*see* Dow 30)
Discipline, 163
Discount brokerages, 57–58
Divergence, 136
Diversification, 22, 26, 37–38, 55, 162
Dividend stocks, 30
Dividends, 32
DJIA (*see* Dow Jones Industrial
    Average)
Dollar, 151
Dollar-cost averaging, 72
Double bottom pattern, 122–124
Double top pattern, 122, 123
Dow, Charles, 10–11
Dow 12, 176
Dow 30 (DIA), 16–17, 85
Dow Jones Industrial Average (DJIA),
    10–11
Dow Jones Transportation Average,
    10–11
Downtrends, 112–113
Dutch tulip bulb mania, 168–169

Earnings estimates, 173
Earnings per share (EPS), 99–100
ECNs (*see* Electronic Communication
    Networks)
Economic indicators, 153
EDGAR database (*see* Electronic Data
    Gathering Analysis and Retrieval
    database)
Edgar Online, 93
Electronic Communication Networks
    (ECNs), 62, 64
Electronic Data Gathering Analysis and
    Retrieval (EDGAR) database, 92,
    93
Emotional involvement, 160–161,
    172–173

Environment, 149–155
 deflationary, 153–154
 of dollar, 151
 and economic indicators, 153
 and Federal Reserve System,
  150–151
 inflationary, 152
 political, 154
 and stock prices, 155
EPS (*see* Earnings per share)
Equities, 4
Ericsson, 159
Exchange-traded funds (ETFs), 79–80
Exercising your right to buy, 82
Exhaustion gap, 127

Famous Financial Fiascos (John Train),
  168
Fast trading strategy(-ies), 77–85
 day trading as, 77–78
 ETFs in, 79–80
 market timing as, 78–79
 news-based, 80
 and options, 81–84
 with QQQ, 84–85
 shorting the rallies as, 79
 writing covered calls as, 83–84
Fear, 161, 167
Federal Reserve Board (FRB), 150
Federal Reserve System, 21, 65,
  150–152
Filling the gap, 127
Finances, 166–167, 175
Fixed-income investments, 19–20
Flexibility, 163
Float shares, 44
Following the crowd, 165–166
Foreign investors, 151
Forward P/E, 101
401(k) plans, 22–23, 180, 183
403(b) plans, 180, 183
Fraud, 34–35
FRB (Federal Reserve Board), 150
Full-service brokerage firms, 55–57

Fundamental analysis, 89–96
 annual report in, 95–96
 balance sheet in, 93–94
 and company managers, 92
 concepts behind, 90–95
 definition of, 89
 and earnings estimates, 100
 earnings per share in, 99–100
 income statement in, 97–99
 industry knowledge for, 90–91
 industry leaders identification for,
  91–92
 and insiders, 92–93
 overview of, 90
 problems with, 104
 stock ratios in, 100–103
 and technical analysis, 173–174
Futures exchanges, 138–139

Gaps, 125–127
GARP (growth at a reasonable price),
  73
GDP (gross domestic product), 153
General Electric, 176
"Going on margin," 63–64
Graham, Benjamin, 105
"Greater fool theory," 73–74
Greed, 160–161
Greenspan, Alan, 141
Gross domestic product (GDP), 153
Growth at a reasonable price (GARP), 73
Growth investors/investing, 73, 101
Growth stocks, 31

Head and shoulders pattern, 120–121
Head fakes, 124
Hedge, 81
Hedge funds, 24
Home ownership, 26
Hoover, Herbert, 65
Hope, 161, 171–172
How to Make Money in Stocks (William
  O'Neil), 75–76
Humes, James C., 107

"Identifying the leading company,"
     91–92
In-and-out trading, 180–183
Income statements, 97–99
Income stocks, 30–31
Index funds, 24–25
Industry knowledge, 90–91
Industry leaders, 91–92
Inflation, 15, 152, 153–154
Initial public offerings (IPOs), 45–47
Insider trading, 146
Insiders, 92–93
Intel, 184–185
Interest rates, 21, 150–151, 152
International funds, 180
Internet, 105, 169
Intrinsic value, 31
Investment banking, 184
Investolator, 74
Investors, individual, 4, 8–9, 176–177
Investor's Business Daily, 91, 144
IPOs (*see* Initial public offerings)
IRAs, 23
"Irrational exuberance," 141, 150

Japan, 154
Junk bonds, 21

Kumar, Ashok, 184–185

"Learn everything you can about the
     industry," 90–91
Learning from mistakes, 163–164,
     174–175
Lebed, Jonathon, 160
Lefevre, Edwin, 128
Level II software, 62
Leveraging, 63
Levitt, Arthur, 176
Liabilities, 93, 94
Limit order, 59–60
Line charts, 109–110
Livermore, Jesse, 128–129, 161

Load funds, 24
Losing stock, selling, 158

MA (*see* Moving average)
Managers, company, 92
Manipulation, 33
Margin calls, 63–64
Margins, 63–64
Market capitalization, 44–45
Market crash(es):
     of 1929, 65–66, 144, 161
     of 1987, 57, 144, 161
Market makers, 14–15
Market orders, 58–61
Market timing, 78–79, 180–183
Maturity date, 20
The media, 143–144
Meeker, Mary, 101, 184
The Merc (Chicago Mercantile
     Exchange), 139
Minis, 139
Mistake(s), 157–169
     of bad advisors, 164–165
     of emotional involvement, 160–161
     of following the crowd, 165–166
     of lack of discipline/flexibility, 163
     of lack of diversification, 162
     of lack of preparation for the worst,
          166–167
     learning from, 174–175
     of letting winning stocks lose, 159–160
     of missing out/mismanaging money,
          167–168
     of not learning from mistakes,
          163–164
     of not selling losing stocks, 158
Momentum investors, 73–74
Money management, 167–168
Money market funds, 25–26
Moving average (MA), 132–133
Munis, 20
Mutual fund money market accounts,
     180

Mutual fund redemptions, 144
Mutual funds, 22–25, 180–183

NASD (National Association of Securities Dealers), 7
Nasdaq (*see* National Association of Securities Dealers Automated Quotation System)
Nasdaq 100 index (QQQ), 84–85
Nasdaq Composite Index, 12
National Association of Securities Dealers Automated Quotation System (Nasdaq), 6–8, 14–15, 33, 57, 78, 84–85, 150
National Association of Securities Dealers (NASD), 7
Net asset value (NAV), 23–24, 180
Net worth, 93
Netscape, 46
New York, 5–6
New York Stock Exchange (NYSE), 6, 10, 14
News-based trading, 80
Niles, Dan, 185
1929 stock market crash, 65–66, 144, 161
1987 stock market crash, 57, 144, 161
No-load funds, 24
Notes, 20

On-balance volume (OBV), 134–135
O'Neil, William, 75–76, 158
Online brokerage divisions, 56
Online investing, 58
Online traders/trading, 58, 78
Opportunities, 167–168
Options, 81–84
Orders, market:
  going on margin with, 63–64
  placing, 61–62
  routing of, 62–63
  types of, 58–61
Oscillators, 137–138

OTC (over-the-counter) market, 33
Outstanding shares, 43–44
Over-the-counter (OTC) market, 33
Overbought, 135
Oversold, 135

P/E ratio (*see* Price/earnings ratio)
P/S (price-to-sales) ratio, 103
Pacific Stock Exchange, 7
Patterns, stock, 119–125
  double bottom, 122–124
  double top, 122, 123
  gaps in, 125–127
  head and shoulders, 120–121
  reverse head and shoulders, 121–122
  triple top, 122
PEG (price/earnings/growth) ratio, 102
Penalties, market-timing, 182
Penny stocks, 33–34
Philadelphia Stock Exchange, 7
Piecyk, Walter, 183
Pink sheet stocks, 33
Points, 12–13
Politics, 154
Portfolios, 37
Position trading, 78
PPI (producer price index), 153
Prechter, Robert, 154
Preferred stocks, 5
Premarket, 53
Premiums, 83–84
Preparation for the worst, 166–167, 175
Previous close, 51
Price, stock, 13, 49–53
  reasons for rise/fall in, 155
  and stock quote, 49–52
Price/earnings/growth (PEG) ratio, 102
Price/earnings (P/E) ratio, 100–102
Price-to-sales (P/S) ratio, 103
Priceline, 101, 184
Principal, 21
Producer price index (PPI), 153

Professional traders, 10
Profit, 13–15
Prospectus, 46–47
Psychological indicators, 142–145
Psychology, 172–173
Pump and dump, 145–146
Put options, 81, 82

QQQQ (*see* Nasdaq 100 index)
Qualcomm, 183
Quote, stock, 49–52

Ratings, 21
Ratios, stock, 100–103
Real estate investment, 26–27, 151
Real estate investment trusts (REITs),
    27
Recessions, 153
REITs (real estate investment trusts),
    27
Relative strength, 76
Relative strength indicator (RSI),
    135–137
Reminiscences of a Stock Operator
    (Edwin Lefevre), 128
Resistance, 118–119
Return on equity (ROE), 103
Reversals, trend, 115–116
Reverse head and shoulders pattern,
    121–122
Reverse splits, 41
Risk, 15–16, 20–21, 178
Risk tolerance, 38
ROE (return on equity), 103
Roosevelt, Franklin Delano, 63, 66
RSI (*see* Relative strength indicator)
Russell 2000 index, 12

Santayana, George, 64
Savings, 154
Scams, 145–146
SEC (*see* U.S. Securities and Exchange
    Commission)

Sectors, 11, 29–30
Securities, 4
Selling short, 41–43, 128
Sentiment analysis, 141–145
    and capitulation, 144–145
    and the media, 143–144
    and mutual fund redemptions, 144
    VIX for, 142–143
September 11, 2001 terrorist attacks,
    143
Shareholders, 4
Shareholders' equity, 93, 94
Shares, 4
    float, 44
    outstanding, 43–44
The Shawshank Redemption (film),
    161
Short-term traders, 9, 162
Shorting stocks, 128
Shorting the rallies, 79
Sideways markets, 28
Sideways trends, 114–115
Siegel, Jeremy, 15
Sincere, Charles, 187
60 Minutes, 184
Slow investment strategy(-ies), 69–76
    bottom fishing as, 71–72
    buy-and-hold, 70–71
    buy-on-the dip, 71
    CANSLIM as, 75–76
    contrarian investing as, 74
    dollar-cost averaging as, 72
    growth investing as, 73
    momentum investing as, 73–74
    value investing as, 72–73
Small Order Execution System (SOES),
    57
Smith, Gary, 180
SOES (Small Order Execution System),
    57
S&P 500 (SPY), 85
S&P (Standard & Poor's Corporation),
    12

Specialists, 14, 62
Split-adjusted prices, 42
Spread, 51–52
SPY (S&P 500), 85
"Stale pricing," 180, 183
Standard & Poor's Corporation (S&P), 12
Stock analysis, 100
Stock certificates, 4–5
Stock charts, 108–109
Stock exchanges, 6–8
Stock market, 3–17
    corporate influence on, 8
    crashes of (see Crash[es], market)
    exchanges for, 6–8
    history of, 5–6
    individual investors in, 8–9
    professional traders in, 10
    and shares, 4
    short-term traders in, 9
    and stock certificates, 4–5
    tracking the, 10–13
Stock patterns (see Patterns, stock)
Stock price (see Price, stock)
Stock quote, 49–52
Stock splits, 40–41
Stockbrokers, 56
Stocks:
    cost of, 13
    definition of, 4
    dividend, 32
    growth, 31
    income, 30–31
    market capitalization of, 44–45
    penny, 33–34
    profit from, 13–15
    reasons for buying, 5, 15
    risk with, 15–16
    and sectors, 29–30
    types of, 29–35
    value, 31
    (See also Shares)
Stop limit order, 61

Stop-loss order, 60–61
Strategy(-ies), 9
    fast trading, 77–85
    guidelines for, 69–70
    slow investment, 69–76
    successful, 179–183
Supply and demand, 155
Support, 116–118
Swing trading, 78
"Swiss cheese principle," 168

Take on the Street (Arthur Levitt), 176
"Talking to company managers," 92
Tax-deferred retirement plans, 22–23, 180, 183
Technical analysis, 107–129
    advanced indicators/oscillators in, 132–138
    bar charts for, 110–111
    candlestick charts for, 111, 112
    definition of, 108
    and fundamental analysis, 173–174
    and gaps, 125–127
    line charts for, 109–110
    problems with, 127
    stock charts for, 108–109
    stock patterns in, 119–125
    support and resistance in, 116–119
    trend lines for, 111–116
    volume in, 131–132
Technical analysts, 108
Technical indicators, 132–137
10–K filing, 93
10–Q filing, 93
TheGlobe.com, 46
Time-zone trading, 180–183
Top line, 97
Tracking the market, 10–13
Trailing P/E, 101
Train, John, 168
Trend reversals, 115–116

Trends, 11, 111–116
  down-, 112–113
  sideways, 114–115
  up-, 113–114
Triple top pattern, 122
Tulip bulb mania, 168–169

Unemployment report, 153
Uptick, 42
Uptrends, 113–114
U.S. Department of Labor, 153
U.S. Securities and Exchange Commission (SEC), 34–35, 47, 63, 66, 92, 146, 185
U.S. Treasuries, 20, 25–26, 166

VA Linux, 46
Value investors, 72–73, 101
Value Line Investment Survey, 91

Value stocks, 31
VIX (*see* Chicago Board Options Exchange Volatility Index)
Volume, 33, 131–132

Wall Street, 6
Wall Street Journal (WSJ), 11
Warren, Ted, 74, 159
Weiss, Martin D., 176
"Whisper number," 100
Wilshire 5000, 12
Winning stocks, losing from, 159–160
Writing covered calls, 83–84
WSJ (*see Wall Street Journal*)

Yield, 20

Zweig, Jason, 180, 182, 183

About the Author

Michael Sincere began trading stocks through the Internet in 1995. Because he wanted to learn more about the stock market, he interviewed some of the top financial experts in the country. He decided to write a book about what he learned; the result was *101 Investment Lessons from the Wizards of Wall Street* (Career Press, 1999).

For his second book, *The Long-Term Day Trader* (Career Press, 2000), coauthored with Deron Wagner, Sincere explained the aggressive investment strategies he helped develop. His third book, *The After-Hours Trader* (McGraw-Hill, 2000), helps investors and traders understand and profit from the high-octane world of after-hours trading.

Sincere has written a number of columns and magazine articles on investing and trading. He has been interviewed on dozens of national radio programs and has appeared on financial news programs, including CNBC and ABC's *World News Now!* to explain his trading strategies and talk about his books.

Sincere's most recent book, *Understanding Options* (McGraw-Hill, 2006), shows that options are easier to understand and less risky than many people believe.

You can e-mail the author at msincere@gmail.com or visit his Web site at www.michaelsincere.com.